Women in Politics

Madeleine Albright

Benazir Bhutto

Hillary Rodham Clinton

Elizabeth Dole

Nancy Pelosi

Queen Noor

WOMEN in POLITICS

Hillary
Rodham Clinton

Heather Lehr Wagner

CHELSEA HOUSE
P U B L I S H E R S
A Haights Cross Communications Company
Philadelphia

CHELSEA HOUSE PUBLISHERS

VP, NEW PRODUCT DEVELOPMENT Sally Cheney
DIRECTOR OF PRODUCTION Kim Shinners
CREATIVE MANAGER Takeshi Takahashi
MANUFACTURING MANAGER Diann Grasse

Staff for **HILLARY RODHAM CLINTON**

EXECUTIVE EDITOR Lee Marcott
ASSOCIATE EDITOR Kate Sullivan
PRODUCTION EDITOR Megan Emery
PHOTO EDITOR Sarah Bloom
SERIES & COVER DESIGNER Terry Mallon
LAYOUT 21st Century Publishing and Communications, Inc.

A Haights Cross Communications ⌖ Company

www.chelseahouse.com

First Printing

9 8 7 6 5 4 3 2 1

Library of Congress Cataloging-in-Publication Data

Wagner, Heather Lehr.
  Hillary Rodham Clinton / by Heather Lehr Wagner.
    v. cm. — (Women in politics)
  Includes index.
  Contents: New York triumph — Preparing for excellence, 1947-1965 — A young
Democrat, 1965-1973 — Bill Clinton and Arkansas, 1973-1982 — From the governor's
mansion to the White House, 1982-1992 — The healthcare debacle, 1992-1994 —
Scandals and hope, 1994-1998 — Senator Clinton.
  ISBN 0-7910-7735-7 — ISBN 0-7910-7999-6 (pbk.)
  1. Clinton, Hillary Rodham—Juvenile literature. 2. Presidents' spouses—United
States—Biography—Juvenile literature. 3. Women legislators—United States—
Biography—Juvenile literature. 4. Legislators—United States—Biography—
Juvenile literature. 5. United States. Congress. Senate—Biography—Juvenile literature.
[1. Clinton, Hillary Rodham. 2. First ladies. 3. Legislators. 4. Women—Biography.]
I. Title. II. Series.
  E887.C55W34 2004
  328.73'092—dc22

                                                              2003025620

Table of Contents

Hillary Rodham Clinton

1

New York Triumph

Women are always being tested . . . but ultimately, each of us has to define who we are individually and then do the very best job we can to grow into it.

—Hillary Rodham Clinton, *Living History*

On November 7, 2000, shortly after 11:00 P.M., a blonde woman strode to the microphones placed at the front of the ballroom of the Grand Hyatt Hotel near Grand Central Station in New York City. The ballroom was crowded with friends and supporters who hugged her or reached out for a handshake as she moved to the podium. Standing by her side were her husband, her daughter, and her mother as she told the cheering crowd, "Sixty-two counties, sixteen months, three debates, two opponents, and six black pantsuits later, because of you, here we are." [1] At the age of 53, Hillary Rodham Clinton had become a United States senator, representing the state of New York.

On November 7, 2000, after supporting her husband's political career for 25 years, Hillary Rodham Clinton finally experienced political success for herself when she was elected a senator for New York State. Hillary's election was remarkable on two accounts: It was the first time a woman had been elected to the U.S. Senate from New York, and it was the first time a former First Lady had been elected to public office.

The election victory marked an end and a beginning for Hillary Rodham Clinton. For 25 years, she had been a political spouse, supporting her husband, Bill Clinton, through his own campaigns for Congress, attorney general of Arkansas, governor of Arkansas, and finally president of the United States. She had spent the past eight years working tirelessly to promote the issues that mattered to her—healthcare reform, women's rights, policies affecting children and families—working without a formal portfolio, shaping the role of First Lady to reflect the needs and aspirations of a new generation of women. She had endured harsh personal and professional criticism, had seen her friends become the targets of rumors and investigations, had been subjected to relentless scrutiny, and had been called before a grand jury to testify about events that had happened years earlier. She had suffered the deaths of a parent and several close friends. She had been publicly embarrassed when revelations about her husband's infidelity became international news and led to an impeachment trial. Her family life, her work as an attorney, her beliefs and ideals, her published writings, her friendships, and even her hairstyles had been intensely analyzed.

On that election night, however, Hillary Rodham Clinton could finally bask in success and approval. The state of New York had chosen her to be one of its representatives in the United States Senate.

The election marked the first time that a woman from New York had been elected to the U.S. Senate. Perhaps more important, it marked the first time in American history that a former First Lady had been elected to public office.

The 16-month campaign, the 8 years as First Lady, and the 25 years spent campaigning for her husband had all shaped the new senator. It had not been an easy transformation. Hillary Rodham Clinton passionately believed that she could make a difference and throughout her life had witnessed the possibilities created by strong, fearless women.

As First Lady, she had saluted her fellow pioneers in a speech at the Vital Voices Conference on Women and Democracy in Reykjavik, Iceland, in October 1999:

> At the end of the day, as we look back on an individual life, or the life of a country, we count how far we have come by many different means. We look at our accomplishments, we admire our art and our culture, we certainly enjoy the successes that we might have. Perhaps the most telling way is whether, generation after generation, we have made the journey less difficult and dangerous for our children.[2]

James Carville, campaign advisor to both Bill and Hillary Clinton, noted that those who thought that they knew Hillary, those who claimed to understand her motives and ambitions, were frequently mistaken. "She is smart, she is aggressive, she can be tough, she likes to bring things to a decision," Carville said. He continued:

> . . . Yet the Hillary Clinton few people know is the woman who never misses a staff party, who knows the names of all my seven brothers and sisters, who never fails to stop and talk with my mother when she sees her. In a world where lots of people move great distances to get away from their parents, Hillary Clinton moved her mother and father from the north side of Chicago to Little Rock, where she and her family could spend time with them. Best of all, Mrs. Clinton has never in any way, shape or form allowed her daughter to be used for any kind of political exploitation. My quarrel with the portrayal of Hillary is not that what people are saying is wrong, it's that there's a whole other side to her that isn't even being discussed. She's an admirable woman.[3]

Carville's "admirable woman" chose to end her autobiography, *Living History,* at the point when she left the White House for the final time, saying her good-byes and even taking a final waltz down the hall with her husband before she began her career in the Senate. Her election to the Senate marked not the end but a new chapter in her career. From her childhood in Park Ridge to her college and law school years, to life in Arkansas and Washington, Hillary Rodham Clinton has always aspired to make a difference.

2

Preparing for Excellence

1947–1965

My family, like every family I know of, was far from perfect. But however imperfect we were, as individuals and as a unit, we were bound together by a sense of commitment and security. My mother and father did what parents do best: They dedicated their time, energy, and money to their children and made sacrifices to give us a better life.

—Hillary Rodham Clinton[1]

Hillary Rodham Clinton's memories of her childhood are full of happy moments of a peaceful life spent with a loving family in Park Ridge, Illinois. She was born on October 26, 1947, to Dorothy and Hugh Rodham. Hillary's memories are all the more poignant because of her awareness that the life her parents provided for her and her two brothers was quite different from the childhoods her parents had experienced.

Hugh Rodham, Hillary's father, grew up in Scranton,

Pennsylvania, in a family crippled by the Great Depression. The stories of his childhood that he shared with Hillary and her brothers involved the young Hugh spending time at the local coal mines, where he would work with the mules that had been blinded by spending too much time underground. Hugh also told of jumping onto slow-moving freight trains and hitching a quick ride, once traveling as far as Binghamton, New York. One family legend involved another stolen ride, this time on an ice truck. Hugh jumped onto the back of the ice truck, but while hanging on to the truck's rear, he was rammed from behind. His lower legs and feet were broken, and doctors planned to amputate both his feet before his mother intervened and refused to allow anyone but her brother-in-law, a simple country doctor, to care for Hugh. He ultimately saved his nephew's legs.

The family stories paint a picture of a fearless, adventurous young boy. Much of Hugh Rodham's fearlessness was shaped by necessity and by family example. His grandmother Isabella, Hillary' great-grandmother, had traveled with her eight children from Wales in the United Kingdom to Scranton, Pennsylvania, in 1882 to join her husband, a worker in the anthracite mines, and build a better life for her family. Hillary's grandfather, also named Hugh, went to work in a Scranton lace mill when he was 13 and worked there for 50 years. Hillary's father also worked in the mines and then stacked boxes in a factory to pay for college. He graduated from Pennsylvania State University in 1935 with a degree in physical education.

Few jobs were available in Scranton in 1935, so Hugh initially found himself following in his family's tradition of working in the mines. Later, he got a job at the Scranton Lace Company before jumping once more on a train and riding it to Chicago, where he found a higher-paying job selling curtains throughout the Midwest for the Columbia Lace Company. There he met Dorothy Howell when she applied for a secretarial job.

Hugh's strength and ambition came from family example. Dorothy Howell, Hillary's mother, had learned to be self-reliant because of a complete absence of family role modeling. Her mother was only 15 and her father only 17 when Dorothy was born, and they divorced when she was eight years old. By then, Dorothy had a five-year-old sister, and when their parents separated, the two young girls were sent alone by train from Chicago, Illinois, to Alhambra, California, to live with their grandparents. The idea of an eight-year-old and a five-year-old being sent on such a long journey by themselves, with Dorothy somehow trying to look after her five-year-old sister, horrified Hillary when she first heard the story. The journey's end brought little relief. Their father's mother harshly disciplined the girls, and their grandfather essentially ignored them. They saw their father rarely, and their mother not at all for ten years.

Dorothy found only a few instances of kindness in her young life. A teacher bought an extra carton of milk each day to give to Dorothy, claiming that she was too full to drink it. A great-aunt gave her gifts and occasionally protected her from her grand-mother's strictness. These few examples of kindness, however, were not enough to make Dorothy's life much better. At the age of 14, Dorothy finally escaped from her grandparents' home and became a live-in nanny for a kind family. She was given room, board, and time to attend high school in exchange for caring for the family's children. The family also gave her books to read and encouraged her in her efforts to become better educated.

After high school, Dorothy left California and moved back to Chicago, where she worked as a secretary. It was when she applied for a job with the Columbia Lace Factory that she met a burly, self-confident salesman named Hugh Rodham. Rodham joined the navy shortly after Pearl Harbor, and he and Dorothy exchanged letters while he was in the service. Rodham became a chief petty officer and, because of his degree in physical education, was give a local assignment, training recruits in physical fitness at Great Lakes Naval Base outside Chicago. Hugh and Dorothy dated and corresponded for five years, finally marrying in 1942.

The young couple lived in a series of apartments in Chicago during the early years of their marriage. Their first child, a daughter, was born in Chicago in 1947. Mrs. Rodham chose her daughter's name, Hillary—a name that at the time was considered a man's name—because she thought it sounded "exotic."[2]

Dorothy decided that her daughter would have a very different childhood from the one she had known. "I was determined that no daughter of mine was going to have to go through the agony of being afraid to say what she had on her mind," Dorothy said in an interview many years later.[3]

After being discharged from the navy, Hugh worked as a salesman and then set up his own custom drapery business. He took orders for draperies from hotels, businesses, and airlines, then printed and sewed the fabric himself. The family saved every dollar it could, living in a one-bedroom apartment in Chicago even after another child, Hugh Junior, was born in 1950.

Finally, after saving up enough money so that they could purchase a home with cash (Hugh Rodham did not believe in mortgages or credit), the family left Chicago and moved to Park Ridge, a suburb northwest of Chicago, into a yellow-brick, Georgian-style home in a conservative community of professional people.

THE FIRST BATTLE

The Rodhams, like many of their neighbors, had chosen to move to Park Ridge to provide their children with a better, safer environment in which to grow, but the move was difficult for four-year-old Hillary, who quickly had to fight for acceptance. In her book *It Takes a Village,* Hillary remembered leaving the house each day "with a bow in my hair and a hopeful look on my face."[4] Going outside to play, she was soon surrounded by the neighborhood kids, who teased her, pushed her, and knocked her down until she burst into tears and ran back into her house.

One girl in particular, a girl named Suzy, took delight in tormenting four-year-old Hillary. Finally, after several weeks,

Hillary's mother met her at the door as she ran back inside in tears. "There's no room in this house for cowards," Dorothy said. "The next time she hits you, I want you to hit her back."[5] Hillary went back outside, shocking the other children. When Suzy began to tease her again, Hillary followed her mother's advice and knocked Suzy down. "I can play with the boys now," Hillary triumphantly informed her mother.[6]

In 1954, Hillary's second brother, Anthony, was born. Hillary remembered her father being stricter with his sons than with her, but Hugh Rodham had high expectations for all of his children, and he wanted them to appreciate the life they enjoyed—a life far easier than the one he had known. Hillary remembered, "'You will never know how lucky you are' was a phrase I heard more times than I can count. He and the fathers of most of my friends were men who had paid their dues and then devoted their energies to giving their families the financial security they themselves had missed."[7]

Hillary's father occasionally drove his children to an impoverished part of Chicago to illustrate this lesson. He pushed his children constantly to achieve higher and higher goals. When Hillary received straight As in junior high school, her father's response was, "Well, Hillary, that must be an easy school you go to."[8]

But Hugh was fond of his children, and in the morning, before work, he sat at the kitchen table helping them with their math homework. He took Hillary and her brothers ice-skating on the Des Plaines River and played pinochle with them at night. He was close to his parents as well, and every August, the Rodham family traveled to Lake Winola, outside Scranton, where they stayed at the Rodham cottage. Hillary's grandfather's cottage had no hot water, no indoor bath or shower. Instead, Hillary and her brothers swam in the Susquehanna River and explored the nearby mountain or fished.

The extended family would sit on the cottage porch, playing cards and talking. Hillary loved hearing her grandfather's stories of traveling to America from Wales as a young boy and working in the lace mills at the age of 11. He shared family lore of the Rodhams' experiences in England and Wales, and Hillary later remembered these as some of the best times she ever had with her father.

EARLY EXCELLENCE

Hugh Rodham traveled into Chicago each day to provide a comfortable living for his family, and Dorothy Rodham enjoyed the traditional mother's role of the 1950s: She stayed at home, caring for her children and the house. When Hugh Rodham put pressure on his children to excel, Dorothy offered affection and gentler encouragement. She attended every school event and every sports event, helped out at the school, and was at home waiting when her children came home for lunch or at the end of the school day.

Dorothy had retained her hard-won interest in education and enjoyed discussing the events of the school day with her children and helping them with research papers and projects. Before Hillary started first grade, her mother spoke of school as a wonderful place where she could begin to make her dreams come true. Dorothy later remembered telling her daughter, "She was going to learn great things, live new passions. I motivated her in a way that she wasn't resigned to go to school. I wanted her to be excited by the idea." [9]

Hillary did enjoy school. She was disciplined and hard-working. She was not terribly athletic, but when she was disappointed at her performance on the school softball team, she and her father spent hours practicing in the park until she could hit a curveball. She earned a wide assortment of merit badges as a Girl Scout and also played soccer and tennis. As she got older, she held part-time jobs as a babysitter and lifeguard. Hillary was not the top student in her competitive public school, but she was on the honor roll and she earned a reputation as a serious and smart girl.

FOCUS ON EDUCATION

Hillary Rodham Clinton's parents emphasized the value of education, and when she became a senator, she focused on increasing the quality of education and instruction available to New York's children.

On March 7, 2001, she stood on the floor of the U.S. Senate and introduced The National Teacher and Principal Recruitment Act:

> . . . My legislation will create a National Teacher Corps that can bring up to 75,000 talented teachers a year into the schools that need them the most. The National Teacher Corps can make the teaching profession more attractive to talented people in our society in several ways. One is by providing bonuses for mid-career professionals interested in becoming teachers. . . . The National Teacher Corps will also make more scholarships available for college and graduate students, and create new career ladders for teacher aides—to become fully certified teachers. And it will ensure that new teachers get the support and professional development they need both to become—and remain—effective teachers.
>
> This bill will also create a national teacher recruitment campaign to provide good information to prospective teachers about resources and routes to teaching through a National Teacher Recruitment Clearinghouse.
>
> And, finally, the bill will create a National Principal Corps to help bring more highly qualified individuals into our neediest schools. . .
>
> I am introducing this bill to make sure that all teachers who step into classrooms and all principals who step into leadership in their schools have the expertise, the knowledge, and the support they need to meet the highest possible standards for all of our children, who deserve nothing less.*

---

* Hillary Rodham Clinton, "Floor Remarks to Introduce the National Teacher and Principal Recruitment Act," March 7, 2001.
  http://clinton.senate.gov/~clinton/speeches/

Hillary was a serious and ambitious student, undoubtedly a result of her parents' influence, who impressed upon her the importance of education from an early age. Hillary, pictured here in her sixth-grade class photo, demonstrated not only scholastic aptitude, but also strong leadership abilities. She was vice president of her junior class, organized babysitting for migrant workers, and was active in her church.

After she became First Lady, Hillary was remembered by classmates as ambitious but fun loving. She was remembered for not worrying too much about her appearance although she was apparently self-conscious about the thick, red-framed glasses she wore to correct her poor eyesight. When running for class office she took off her glasses but then needed a friend to steer her down the halls and point out people they knew.

Two older mentors played an important role in Hillary's early political development. Her ninth-grade history teacher, Paul Carlson, drilled his students on the evils of Communism, telling stories of the heroic exploits of General Douglas MacArthur. He encouraged Hillary and her classmates to take a conservative view of political events in the 1950s and early 1960s, a view supported by Hillary's father, a staunch Republican.

The Methodist Church also played an important role in the Rodham family life, and Hillary and her brothers attended Sunday school and participated in youth groups and other church activities. Hillary later said that it was through the church that she was first exposed to the world that existed beyond her all-white, middle-class suburb. At a time that the civil rights movement was beginning to receive more widespread awareness, Hillary noted, "My church gave me concrete experiences that forced me to confront the reality of inequity and injustice." [10]

The youth minister of First Methodist, Reverend Don Jones, helped develop the church's outreach programs and exposed Hillary and the other young members of the congregation to African-American and Hispanic teenagers, driving them to service and worship exchanges in downtown Chicago. When Martin Luther King, Jr., came to Chicago to speak, Reverend Jones arranged for Hillary and some other church members to meet him.

Hillary's family was active in the church's outreach programs. Her mother organized a summer Bible school that worked with Mexican migrant workers who arrived each summer to provide inexpensive labor to nearby farmers. Hillary, at the age of 14, organized a group of older students from the Bible school to provide babysitting for the farm workers' children, who were often forced to spend the day home alone while their parents worked.

CAMPAIGNS AND COLLEGE PLANS

Both her history teacher and her youth minister provided Hillary with exposure to dramatically different ideas. That both would later remember her as a dedicated supporter of many of their own ideals demonstrates how eager Hillary was to learn—and how skilled she was at embracing different philosophies and bringing them together in a way that made sense to her.

Many of the memories that focus on life in the 1950s and 1960s reflect a longing for what is described as a simpler, safer time. Hillary's memories of her childhood and young adulthood are balanced by an awareness that life was far from perfect then. "Ask African-American children who grew up in a segregated society," she writes in her book *It Takes a Village*, "or immigrants who struggled to survive in sweatshops and tenements, or women whose life choices were circumscribed and whose work was underpaid."[11] Hillary's own understanding of the limits that society placed on her came at the age of 14. She was fascinated by astronauts and space travel and wrote to NASA asking what it took to be an astronaut. She was told that girls should not apply.[12]

Hillary, however, did not believe that her gender should limit her options. She ran for election as vice president of her junior class and won. In her senior year, she ran for senior class president but was defeated after her two male opponents used what she later remembered as mudslinging and dirty campaign tactics. Disappointed by the defeat, she turned her attention to what would come after high school.

Most of the other students in Hillary's high school planned to attend the University of Illinois or other local colleges. Hillary wanted something better. A young teacher at Hillary's high school had told her that women's colleges, such as Vassar, Wellesley, and Radcliffe, were the best for women (at the time, the elite Ivy League schools like Dartmouth, Yale, Harvard, and Princeton did not accept women), so she applied and was accepted to all three.

Hillary ultimately chose Wellesley College, a school 1,000 miles from Park Ridge. A government teacher cautioned her that the liberal atmosphere of the college would turn her into a Democrat. "I'm smart," Hillary replied. "I know where I stand on the issues. And that's not going to change."[13]

A Young Democrat

1965–1973

We know that to be educated, the goal of it must be human liberation—
liberation enabling each of us to fulfill our capacity so as to be free to
create within and around ourselves.
—Hillary Rodham Clinton, Wellesley College Commencement Speech

At the beginning, Hillary struggled to find her place at Wellesley. She had thought that perhaps she might become a scientist or a doctor, but freshman courses in math and geology convinced her otherwise. Many of her classmates came from wealthy families and had traveled abroad. She felt lonely and out of place.

Within a month, she called home, telling her parents that she wasn't smart enough for Wellesley. Her father told her to come home, but her mother told her that she didn't want her daughter to be a "quitter." [1]

Gradually, Hillary began to find her niche in the challenging academic environment. At the time Hillary attended college, the expectations for women in the United States were undergoing dramatic changes. Previous classes graduating from Wellesley had focused as much on finding a husband as finding a career. During Hillary's four years of college, the feminist movement was beginning to take root in America, encouraging women to view themselves in a larger context than simply as wife and mother. Wellesley's Latin motto—*Non Ministrari sed Ministrare* (Not to be ministered to, but to minister)—took on new meaning for young women seeking to make a difference in the world.

For Hillary, the transformation would prove political as well. During her freshman year, she was elected president of the college's Young Republicans organization. As she learned more about the Vietnam War and the civil rights movement, she began to question many of the ideas and beliefs that had previously shaped her political thinking. She began to read the *New York Times*. She was challenged by political science professors to expand her sources of information. Eventually, she recognized that her thinking had shifted so dramatically that she needed to step down as president of the Young Republicans.

Current events further affected Hillary's thinking. The year 1968 was a dramatic one in American history: President Lyndon Johnson decided not to seek another term in office; Martin Luther King, Jr. was assassinated; and Robert Kennedy was assassinated. By the time of her junior year, Hillary's political position had shifted: the former president of the Young Republicans became an ardent supporter of presidential candidate Eugene McCarthy, a Democratic senator (and antiwar activist) from Minnesota. On weekends, Hillary traveled from Wellesley to Manchester, New Hampshire, to volunteer at McCarthy's campaign headquarters, where she eventually met the candidate himself.

Hillary was elected college government president in 1968, at a point when protests over Martin Luther King, Jr.'s assassination were forcing dramatic changes across the country. An all-campus meeting was held at Wellesley, and Hillary was asked to help bridge the gap between African-American students and campus officials.

At Wellesley College, Hillary's political beliefs began to shift toward those of the Democratic Party. She became involved in politics on a national level, volunteering on the presidential campaign for Democrat Eugene McCarthy, and on a collegiate level, serving as student body president. Here, Hillary is pictured between two other Wellesley students at the college's government election in February 1968.

HILLARY GOES TO WASHINGTON

In the summer of 1968, Hillary traveled to Washington, D.C., for the nine-week Wellesley Internship Program. She was assigned to intern at the House Republican Conference and worked with a group headed by then Minority Leader (and later U.S. president) Gerald Ford. The group also included Congressman Charles Goodell from New York, who encouraged Hillary and several other interns to travel to the Republican Convention in Miami to work on behalf of Governor Nelson Rockefeller of New York, who was attempting to take the presidential nomination away from Richard Nixon.

Hillary traveled to Miami, where she worked in the busy Rockefeller for President suite, answering phone calls and carrying messages to and from the convention. Nixon won the nomination, and Hillary returned from Florida convinced that she could not support the Republican Party's more conservative ideology.

Back home in Park Ridge, she was soon inspired to attend another convention: the Democratic Convention in nearby Chicago. Hillary's parents were out of town and could not object to their daughter's decision to attend a political gathering marked by protests and police brutality. What Hillary saw deeply shocked her. Police officers brandishing nightsticks, protestors throwing rocks, the smell of tear gas, and the noise of screamed obscenities all made it clear that a very different America existed from the one she had seen in the safe environments of Park Ridge and Wellesley.

During her senior year, Hillary decided that she wanted to make a difference in the world, but unlike many of the activists she had read about and studied, Hillary believed that protest could work from the inside, instead of only from the outside. She decided to go to law school.

She applied to and was accepted by both Harvard University and Yale University. A trip to Harvard helped her make her choice. She was introduced to a Harvard law professor by a male law student, who explained that Hillary was trying to choose between Harvard and its "closest competitor." The professor studied her coolly, and then said, "Well, first of all, we don't have any close competitors. Secondly, we don't need any more women at Harvard."[2] Hillary decided to attend Yale.

A MILESTONE

As Hillary and her classmates were completing their senior year, Wellesley president Ruth Adams was approached by a group of students asking that a member of the class of 1969 be allowed to give a commencement speech. The college's administration had already invited Republican senator Edward Brooke to give the commencement speech, so Adams refused the unprecedented request for a student speaker.

The students decided to stage an alternative commencement and asked Hillary to be the speaker, but Hillary instead went to Adams, asking her to explain her objections to the idea of a student speaker. Adams replied that it had never been done before and that she didn't know who the speaker would be. When Hillary responded that she had been the student invited to speak, Adams eventually agreed—only a few days before the graduation ceremony.

Hillary frantically set to work preparing her speech, barraged by suggestions of themes, poems, and quotes from friends. Her mother was sick and unable to attend the ceremony, but on learning that his daughter was speaking at her graduation, Hugh Rodham flew to Massachusetts.

On May 31, 1969, as the students and their guests gathered on Wellesley's Academic Quadrangle for the commencement ceremonies, Hillary was still revising her speech. In the end, she used some of what she had prepared in those last frantic days and also added remarks directly responding to Senator Brooke's speech, which came before hers.

Hillary listened to the senator talk about the profound social problems facing America, listened as he argued against protest without mentioning Vietnam or civil rights or the questions young people had about their nation's leadership. "His words," Hillary later noted, "were aimed at a different Wellesley, one that predated the upheavals of the 1960s."[3]

When it was Hillary's turn, she rose before the crowd of approximately 2,000; she spoke for about ten minutes without notes, describing the difference between the expectations she and her 400 classmates had when they first came to Wellesley and the reality they had witnessed during the past four years. She defended protests as a way to forge an identity; she spoke of her classmates' fears about the future. At the end, she paraphrased a classmate's poem, saying, "The challenge now is to practice politics as the art of making what appears to be impossible, possible."[4]

The response was a standing ovation from her classmates

that lasted for seven minutes. One of Hillary's classmates remembered the speech—and their four years at Wellesley—as an evolution for themselves and their college: "When we started Wellesley, it was a girls' school," she said. "When we left it had become a women's college."[5]

Hillary's speech was included in a collection of student commencement speeches published in *Life* magazine that year. The speeches were published with a response by Vice President Spiro Agnew, who noted that students should reject "violent rebellion" and "immature dissent" and instead accept the "rational" status quo: "Ask yourselves which kind of society you want for tomorrow—tomorrow, when you are the establishment."[6] Agnew would be forced out of office in four years in a bribery scandal.

YALE LAW SCHOOL

There were 235 first-year students entering Yale Law School in the fall of 1969. Hillary was one of 27 women in the group, a small percentage by contemporary standards, but in the late 1960s, a truly significant number. Hillary Rodham was one of many law students at Yale interested in a career in public service, and the courses and campus fostered an environment in which students were encouraged not merely to study the philosophy of law in a remote classroom but to actively practice what they were studying in the "real world."

The "real world" as it existed in the New Haven outside of Yale's campus was caught up in the climate of social change sweeping across the country. In April 1970, during Hillary's second semester at Yale, demonstrations broke out in New Haven, prompted by the trial of eight members of the African-American activist group the Black Panthers for murder. Yale's law library, located in the basement of the law school, was set on fire on April 27. Hillary was one of hundreds of students, faculty, and staff who hurried to extinguish the flames and attempted to save the library's valuable collection. Security patrols, composed largely of students, were organized to maintain a 24-hour watch over the library for the remainder of that year.

Other national events marked Hillary's first year of law school. In April 1970, President Nixon expanded the Vietnam War by sending additional American troops into Cambodia. On May 4, National Guard troops in Ohio, reacting to student protests on the campus of Kent State University, opened fire and killed four students.

Because her commencement speech from Wellesley had been published in *Life,* Hillary was invited to speak before the convention banquet of the League of Women Voters as they celebrated their 50th anniversary in Washington, D.C., in May 1970. Hillary had approached her law school studies seriously, but the political events of that first year had stirred her deeply. When she delivered the speech, she wore a black armband in tribute to the students who had been killed only days earlier at Kent State.

"Here we are on the other side of a decade that had begun with a plea for nobility and ended with the enshrinement of mediocrity," Hillary's speech noted. She described the sense of her generation that they had been presented with a "chain of broken promises," and encouraged her audience to take personal responsibility for the social problems impacting life in America:

> Our social indictment has broadened. Where once we advocated civil rights, now we advocate a realignment of political and economic power. Where once we exposed the quality of life in the world of the South and of the ghettos, now we condemn the quality of work in factories and corporations. Where once we assaulted the exploitation of man, now we decry the destruction of nature as well.[7]

Hillary included arguments on why the Vietnam War's expansion into Cambodia was illegal, and offered an explanation for the student protests. The League of Women Voters provided more than a forum for Hillary to demonstrate her skills at speaking before diverse groups: It would also prove an important networking opportunity. At the League of Women Voters meeting, she met several people who would become important contacts, both for her and for her future husband.

The keynote speaker at the convention was Marian Wright Edelman, a Yale Law graduate who had become the first African-American woman admitted to the bar in Mississippi. Edelman was actively involved in the civil rights movement and was working on educational programs in Mississippi. Hillary had met Marian Edelman's husband, Peter Edelman, a year earlier. At the convention, he introduced the two women, and Hillary agreed to join Marian Edelman's Washington Research Project, an antipoverty organization. At the same meeting Hillary was also introduced to Vernon Jordan, director of the Voter Education Project of the Southern Regional Council in Atlanta and a supporter—like Hillary—of the movement to lower the voting age from 21 to 18. Ultimately, the Twenty-sixth Amendment was passed in 1971, sparked in part by arguments that young men who were old enough to fight for their country should be allowed to vote in it and affect its policies. Attorney Vernon Jordan would also prove an important contact for Hillary, and later for Bill Clinton.

The summer after her first year of law school, Hillary volunteered for the Washington Research Project and then worked for Minnesota Senator Walter Mondale's Subcommittee on Migratory Labor. Mondale had formed a committee to study the living and working conditions of migrant farm workers, and Hillary was asked to research the education and health of migrant children, a tie-in from her work for Marian Wright Edelman's Washington Research Project.

It was not Hillary's first exposure to the children of migrant farm workers. As a young teenager, Hillary had worked at a camp for migrant workers—a mission project for her Sunday school—babysitting the children too young to work in the fields with their parents. Now she attended the hearings, gasping in horror as the committee revealed terrible conditions at the migrant camps in Florida and elsewhere, including those run by such prominent corporations as Coca-Cola (through its Minute

MARIAN WRIGHT EDELMAN

While still in law school, Hillary was introduced to Marian Wright Edelman. Hillary later worked with Edelman on her Washington Research Project and the Children's Defense Fund that she founded. Both women shared a passionate commitment to issues involving children and the disadvantaged.

Marian Wright Edelman, like Hillary, was a graduate of Yale Law School. In the mid-1960s she became the first African-American woman admitted to the Mississippi Bar; she also directed the NAACP Legal Defense and Education Fund office in Jackson, Mississippi. In 1968, she moved to Washington, D.C., and worked with Dr. Martin Luther King, Jr. on the Poor People's March he organized before his death. The Washington Research Project she founded functioned as a public interest law firm and later led to the Children's Defense Fund, which she founded in 1973.

The Children's Defense Fund became one of the most effective private, nonprofit groups lobbying on behalf of children, particularly poor and minority children and those with disabilities. It has helped to sponsor programs like Head Start and to encourage public awareness of the needs of children.

Marian Wright Edelman has been honored with numerous awards for her advocacy, including the Albert Schweitzer Humanitarian Prize, the MacArthur Foundation Prize Fellowship, the Robert F. Kennedy Lifetime Achievement Award, and the Presidential Medal of Freedom. "Service is the rent we pay to be living," Edelman has said. "It is the very purpose of life and not something you do in your spare time."*

* About.Com: Women's History, "Marian Wright Edelman Quotations."
 http://womenshistory.about.com/library/qu/blquedel.htm

Maid division). One account says that Hillary accosted the president of Coca-Cola, J. Paul Austin, when he arrived to testify on July 24. "She was really something, this young activist breathing fire," a Coca-Cola lawyer later reported.[8]

SECOND YEAR

Hillary returned to Yale in the fall of 1970 deeply affected by the stories she had heard of the conditions of children in the migrant camps. She decided that the focus of her law studies would be on how the law affected children. Two of her law professors suggested that she spend time at the Yale Child Study Center, where she attended case discussions and observed clinical sessions. She also began work at the New Haven Legal Services office, where she became involved in cases of suspected child abuse and neglect.

Through her work and study, Hillary began to see first-hand cases of domestic violence or child abuse and neglect. Stories of her own mother's difficult childhood deepened her dedication and interest in the area of children's rights. In 1974, the *Harvard Educational Review* published an article by Hillary Rodham, the result of her observations and study of the legal issues surrounding children's rights. Entitled "Children Under the Law," it focused on the appropriate legal action necessary when family situations threatened children's health or welfare. Her position would later be interpreted by critics as an "antifamily" philosophy, but Hillary's thoughts were shaped by an impulse to protect children and provide them with the best hope for a safe future.

In her second year of law school, Hillary met a fellow student who would dramatically alter the course of her life. Walking by the law school's student lounge one day, Hillary saw a tall student, with curly hair and a red-brown beard, talking as a group of students listened: ". . . and not only that, we grow the biggest watermelons in the world!" she heard him say as she walked by.

"Who *is* that?" Hillary asked a friend.

"Oh, that's Bill Clinton," her friend responded. "He's from Arkansas, and that's all he ever talks about."[9]

It would be several more months before Hillary Rodham and Bill Clinton had their first conversation. She had seen him around campus, but it was not until the spring of 1971 that she spoke with the student she described as arriving at Yale "looking more like a Viking than a Rhodes Scholar returning from two years at Oxford."[10] Hillary was studying in the library, and Bill was standing outside in the hall talking to another student when she noticed that he kept looking at her. Finally, Hillary stood up, walked over, and said, "If you're going to keep looking at me, and I'm going to keep looking back, we might as well be introduced. I'm Hillary Rodham."[11]

BILL CLINTON

The young man to whom Hillary introduced herself on that day had come from a background quite different from the stable, secure family life Hillary had known in Park Ridge. He was born on August 19, 1946, and named William Jefferson Blythe. By the time of his birth, his father had already been dead for three months, killed in a car crash. Bill Clinton was raised in Hope, Arkansas, by his maternal grandparents while his mother, Virginia Kelley, attended nursing school in New Orleans.

When Bill was four years old, his mother married Roger Clinton, and the couple and Bill moved into their own home in Hope. Roger Clinton was abusive and an alcoholic. Bill tried to protect his mother and, later, his half-brother Roger, who was ten years younger. In 1953, the family moved to Hot Springs, Arkansas, where Roger Clinton's abusiveness and alcoholism accelerated. Finally, when Bill was 15 years old, he confronted his stepfather and demanded that he stop hitting his mother.

Despite the chaos in his home life, Bill Clinton excelled in school. At the age of 16, he won a nomination to the American Legion's national assembly for boys in Washington, D.C., where he met President John F. Kennedy. The trip changed his life, shifting his focus from a career in medicine to a career in politics and influencing his choice of college: Georgetown University.

Following four years at Georgetown, he was awarded a Rhodes scholarship and traveled to England to attend Oxford University for two years. He arrived at Yale University's Law School with long sideburns in the style of Elvis Presley and a determination to become president of the United States one day.

Hillary Rodham, the serious, studious young woman from the suburbs of Chicago, and Bill Clinton, the handsome, gregarious young man from Arkansas, were a clear case of the principle that "opposites attract." Clinton was always surrounded by a group of students, his warmth and story-telling gifts drawing a crowd wherever he went. Hillary would carefully prepare for classes, studying diligently and working hard, but Bill Clinton was more casual in his approach, waiting until late in the semester and then cramming for his final exams, performing quite well in the end.

The two soon became a couple, driving around New Haven in Clinton's burnt-orange station wagon. Early in their relation-ship, both were equally clear about what the future held for them: Hillary wanted a career in civil rights and child advocacy; Clinton planned to return to Arkansas and run for office.

They spent the summer of 1971 in California. Hillary was clerking at a small law firm in Oakland. Clinton had been invited to work on Senator George McGovern's presidential campaign helping campaign manager Gary Hart organize the southern states. Instead, Clinton decided to go to California to spend more time with Hillary. They shared an apartment near the University of California at Berkeley and spent the weekends exploring nearby San Francisco and Oakland.

When the summer ended, they returned to New Haven, renting a small apartment near Yale's campus. Clinton orga-nized a McGovern for President headquarters in New Haven, drafting Yale students and faculty to help staff the operation. Hillary continued her work at the New Haven Legal Assistance

Association, concentrating on issues surrounding foster care. They studied, entertained friends, and debated political issues. They worked together on a mock trial competition, preparing their arguments and witnesses for an entire semester. Despite their hard work, they lost the competition.

Hillary spent the summer of 1972 working for Marian Wright Edelman again, gathering information about the Nixon administration's failure to enforce school integration. In the southern United States, a large number of private schools had been founded. These schools were segregated. Such schools were legally prevented from receiving tax-exempt status, but President Nixon had failed to take a forceful position on ensuring the ban.

Later, Hillary joined Bill Clinton in Texas, where he was working as part of the George McGovern presidential campaign. Hillary's assignment was to encourage Hispanics in South Texas, as well as the 18-year-olds who had recently been granted the right to vote, to vote for McGovern. One volunteer remembered Hillary's directness and energy: "You couldn't spend five minutes with her without noticing her powerful focus and her drive. She had this raucous humor and incredible laugh—there was a total lack of pomposity." [12]

The McGovern campaign served as a kind of laboratory for both Hillary Rodham and Bill Clinton. Both had volunteered on other campaigns before, but during their time in Texas they could see what worked and what didn't. The McGovern campaign flagged despite revelations about wrongdoings by President Nixon. Hillary studied the situation in Texas, gaining a greater understanding of the operation of a presidential campaign on the local level. After the voter registration effort had ended, Hillary stayed on to help run the campaign in San Antonio during its final month.

Later, Hillary noted that she had learned from the experience in San Antonio that a national campaign must be more responsive to ideas and plans from the local offices. When McGovern finally agreed to make an appearance in San Antonio during the final days of the campaign, Hillary witnessed the interaction between advance staff and the local representatives. "I learned that they [the advance staff] operated under tremendous stress, wanted all the essentials—phones, copiers, a stage, chairs, sound system—to appear yesterday, and that in a tight or a losing race, somebody has to be responsible for paying the bills," she later explained. "Every time the advance team ordered something, they'd tell me the money to pay for it would be wired down immediately. But the money never appeared."[13]

Hillary and Bill took a brief vacation in Mexico, debating the successes and failures of the McGovern campaign while enjoying the warm beaches. They then returned to Yale. Clinton, who had spent two years at Oxford as a Rhodes Scholar, still had one more year of law school. Hillary had completed her course work but decided to stay on at Yale for an additional year, taking classes in legal issues affecting children and working at Yale New Haven Hospital to help the staff develop policies to deal with suspected cases of child abuse.

When they had both finished law school, in the spring of 1973, they traveled together to Europe. Clinton showed Hillary the places he had seen during his time at Oxford, taking her on tours of London, Stonehenge, and Wales. It was while they were in the scenic Lake District that Bill Clinton first asked Hillary Rodham to marry him.

Hillary later remembered being "desperately in love" with the man she described as "a force of nature" but uncertain about her own future. She replied, "No, not now."[14]

In 1991, speaking before an audience in Chautauqua, New York, Hillary described the conflict she felt at the marriage proposal. "We were both very concerned about our country and its direction and fascinated by politics and committed to public service," she said. "We also realized that a marriage between two people like us was never, ever going to be easy, if it could even happen at all. When we graduated from law school, he went right back to Arkansas. I wanted nothing to do with that."[15]

4

Bill Clinton and Arkansas

1973–1982

The challenges of change are always hard. It is important that we begin to unpack those challenges that confront this nation and realize that we each have a role that requires us to change and become more responsible for shaping our own future.

—Hillary Rodham Clinton, *Living History*

Hillary Rodham again took a job with Marian Wright Edelman, joining a staff created as part of Edelman's new Children's Defense Fund (CDF). She moved to Cambridge, Massachusetts, renting an apartment and living alone for the first time in her life. One of the CDF's mandates was to lobby and litigate, representing the interests of poor, minority, and handicapped children at both the state and national level. As a staff attorney for the CDF, Hillary traveled to South Carolina to investigate the conditions under which juveniles were incarcerated in adult jails, helping CDF's efforts to separate juveniles from adult prisoners and providing them with greater protection. In New Bedford, Massachusetts, she worked on a CDF campaign to determine why the census figures of school-aged children and the numbers of children actually enrolled in schools were different. Hillary went door to door, discovering young children who were not attending school because of physical disabilities or, in other cases, because they were at home caring for younger siblings while their parents worked.

The work was rewarding, but Hillary found that she was lonely and missed Bill. He was teaching at the University of Arkansas Law School in Fayetteville and planning his own political future. Demonstrating the conflict she was feeling, Hillary had taken the bar exams for both Arkansas and Washington, D.C., uncertain which direction her career was leading. She passed in Arkansas but failed in Washington. Bill Clinton was planning a run for Congress, but Hillary was not yet willing to give up her own ambitions.

IMPEACHING A PRESIDENT

After less than six months with the CDF, Hillary was restless. Then she received a call from John Doar, the new chief counsel to the House of Representatives' Judiciary Committee. Doar was forming a staff to work on the impeachment inquiry investigating President Nixon. It was a historic opportunity, and even though the pay was low, the hours long, and the work promised to be tedious and painstaking, Hillary quickly accepted. She moved to Washington in January 1974, joining 43 other attorneys and 60 investigators, clerks, and secretaries.

The 26-year-old Hillary Rodham understood the historic importance of the work she had been given. She enthusiastically spent long days and nights in makeshift offices reviewing documents and transcribing tapes. The staff researched the only other presidential impeachment, that of Andrew Johnson, looking for precedents and legal procedures. They worked into the spring and summer, making notes on thousands of index cards, one fact per card, all cross-referenced, slowly and painstakingly compiling the case for the impeachment of President Nixon.

On July 19, 1974, John Doar presented the articles of impeachment that his staff had prepared, outlining the case for the charges against President Nixon. The evidence included paying witnesses to influence their testimony, using the Internal Revenue Service to obtain tax records of private citizens, and using the FBI and the Secret Service to spy on private

WATERGATE

In January 1974, Hillary Rodham Clinton joined the staff formed by the House of Representatives' Judiciary Committee to work on the impeachment inquiry investigating President Richard Nixon. The scandal known as Watergate, which led to the impeachment inquiry, actually began in 1972, when a group of burglars with connections to President Richard Nixon were arrested following a break-in at the Democratic Party's National Committee offices in the Watergate Hotel in Washington, D.C., on June 17. President Nixon was reelected in 1973, but by 1974, the scandal had built to a point that impeachment seemed likely.

The exposure of Watergate was initiated by two reporters from the *Washington Post*, Carl Bernstein and Bob Woodward, who published details of the scandal and its implications for the Nixon administration, basing some of their information on a mysterious contact familiar with events inside the Nixon White House known only as "Deep Throat." The reports soon led to political investigations, which began in February 1973 with a committee established by the Senate to investigate any improprieties on the part of the citizens. Three articles were approved by the House Judiciary Committee—abuse of power, obstruction of justice, and contempt of Congress.

Facing the prospect of a trial in the Senate, Richard Nixon resigned the presidency on August 9, and Hillary Rodham was out of work. Most of her friends believed that she would return to work for the Children's Defense Fund; some thought that she would pursue a career in politics. All were shocked when she announced that instead she had decided to move to Arkansas.

"Are you out of your mind?" one friend, Sara Ehrman, exclaimed at the news. "Why on earth would you throw away your future?" [1] Ehrman offered to drive Hillary to Arkansas,

president. In the public hearings, evidence from White House Counsel John Dean revealed a deeply troubled administration, and the revelation that secret White House tape recordings existed shocked the nation and sparked a legal battle between Congress and the president over access to the tapes.

By 1974, the House of Representatives had authorized its Judiciary Committee to consider impeachment proceedings against President Nixon. The Committee ultimately voted to accept three of four proposed Articles of Impeachment, with many Republicans joining Democrats in their recommendation of impeachment. The Supreme Court then ordered President Nixon to release his White House tapes, which revealed that the president had been involved in the Watergate cover-up.

With impeachment likely, President Nixon chose instead to resign. On August 8, 1974, in a televised speech, he told the nation that he had decided to step down. His vice president, Gerald Ford, became the thirty-eighth president of the United States, later issuing a controversial pardon of Nixon.

stopping periodically to ask her if she knew what she was doing. Hillary's response was always the same: "No, but I'm going anyway."[2]

Hillary Clinton later explained that the decision made sense for her. She missed Bill, they wanted to be together, and when her work in Washington ended, she was the one who had no ties to a particular geographic place and so had the flexibility to move:

> I knew I was happier with Bill than without him, and I'd always assumed that I could live a fulfilling life anywhere. If I was going to grow as a person, I knew it was time for me—to paraphrase Eleanor Roosevelt—to do what I was most afraid to do. So I was driving toward a place where I'd never lived and had no friends or family. But my heart told me I was going in the right direction.[3]

A POLITICAL PARTNERSHIP

Thanks to a few introductions from Bill, and her own impressive resume, Hillary was quickly given an offer to teach at the University of Arkansas Law School. Her assignment was to teach criminal law and trial advocacy, as well as to run the legal aid clinic and prison projects, supervising law students as they provided legal advice to the poor and those in prison. She also quickly became involved in Bill Clinton's congressional campaign, trying to create order and efficiency among the undisciplined volunteers.

Arkansas was a dramatic change from Washington, and even New Haven. Fayetteville was a small college town, where the pace of life was considerably slower. Hillary was one of only two female law professors at the university, and she quickly earned a reputation as a demanding teacher, requiring students to come to class prepared. She was described by some as a "hippie" because of her baggy sweaters, large glasses, and long straight hair. Bill Clinton's mother, Virginia, a woman who spent at least 45 minutes a day applying makeup and doing her hair, was horrified and bewildered by Hillary's appearance and clothing style.

Hillary was determined. She had made a decision to come to Arkansas, and she would not quit. Her brothers and her father arrived in Arkansas and spent several weeks working for Bill Clinton's campaign, pasting signs on trees and fences. Clinton won the primary but lost the election by only 6,000 votes.

Both continued their teaching careers, but for a time it was Hillary whose career was on the rise. She had rented a comfortable, luxurious apartment; she handled several high-profile legal cases and founded the University of Arkansas' first legal aid clinic. At the end of the school year, she decided to take a trip back east to meet with friends, talk to some contacts who were offering her jobs, and decide once and for all where she belonged.

As Clinton drove her to the airport, they passed a small, red brick house near the university with a "For Sale" sign posted on its front lawn. Hillary commented that the house was sweet.

She spent time in Chicago and on the East Coast, wrestling with her career choices. Had Bill Clinton won the congressional election, they could have moved back to Washington. Clinton, however, was now considering running for Arkansas attorney general, a position that paid only $6,000 a year. Hillary understood that she was at a crossroads. If she decided to stay with Bill Clinton, she would be committing to spending at least the next several years in Arkansas and to becoming the partner in their relationship responsible for their financial security. She was still wrestling with her decision when she returned to Arkansas.

Bill met her at the airport and proudly drove up to the house that they had spotted on their drive to the airport several weeks earlier. Hillary had completely forgotten about their conversation and was shocked when he announced that he had bought the home that she liked. "Now you'd better marry me," he said, "because I can't live there all by myself." [4] Hillary finally said "yes."

MARRIED LIFE

Hillary Rodham and Bill Clinton were married in the living room of their new home on October 11, 1975. Her brothers had tried to help paint and fix up the house for the simple ceremony, but paint cans and drop cloths were still covering the house the night before the ceremony, and Hillary had no wedding dress. Her mother took her to a department store where Hillary bought the first dress she saw, a Victorian-style gown made of lace and muslin.

The wedding reception was held in the backyard of the couple's friends, Ann and Morris Henry, where a few hundred people gathered to toast the new couple—and discuss Bill Clinton's prospects in the upcoming race for attorney general. To the horror of Bill Clinton's mother—and the shock of many in Arkansas—Hillary did not take her new husband's name, a fact that was noted in the wedding announcement published in the *Arkansas Democrat-Gazette*. The couple had not planned for a honeymoon, so Hillary's mother purchased tickets for the newlyweds—and the entire Rodham family— for a trip to Acapulco.

Hillary and Bill were so different and came from such different backgrounds that their marriage—and Hillary's decision to move to Arkansas—puzzled many friends. Betsy Wright, who had worked with both Bill and Hillary on the McGovern campaign in Texas, said, "I had images in my mind that she could be the first woman president." [5] Bill Clinton's childhood friend Mack McLarty, who would later serve as his chief of staff in the White House, noted, "I married above myself in terms of intellect, like Bill did." [6]

Even after several decades of marriage, Hillary would be asked about her choice. "All I know is that no one understands me better and no one can make me laugh the way Bill does," she wrote in her autobiography. "Even after all these years, he is still the most interesting, energizing and fully alive person I have ever met. Bill Clinton and I started a conversation in the spring of 1971, and more than thirty years later we're still talking."[7]

MOVE TO LITTLE ROCK

When the couple returned from Mexico, Bill Clinton campaigned aggressively for the state attorney general post, traveling around the state to meet people and garner support. He won the primary in May 1976, and the Republicans did not put up a candidate against him. Knowing that his election was assured, both Bill and Hillary devoted their energy that fall to supporting Democrat Jimmy Carter in his presidential campaign against incumbent Gerald Ford.

Carter had spoken the year before at the University of Arkansas, and both Bill and Hillary had the opportunity to meet him. Bill worked on Carter's campaign in Arkansas while Hillary traveled to Indiana to work as the field coordinator in that heavily Republican state. It was a difficult job because it seemed clear that Carter could not carry Indiana, but Hillary plunged in, helping to draft local people to work under the direction of regional coordinators. As expected, Carter did not win in Indiana, but he won the national election.

With Bill the newly elected attorney general, Hillary now faced a move to the state capital, Little Rock. It was too far from Fayetteville for her to commute, so she was also forced to give up the teaching job she had come to love and the circle of friends she had found there.

Hillary began to consider her career options. She needed to find a position that would not create a conflict of interest for Bill in his role as attorney general, which ruled out any kind of state-funded institution or a public position as a defender, prosecutor, or legal aid attorney. In addition, with her husband earning only a modest salary, she had to consider a position that would contribute to their financial security.

Joining a private law firm became the most logical choice. After the election, Hillary was approached by Vince Foster and Herbert Rule, two partners of the prestigious Rose, Nash, Williamson, Carroll, Clay, and Giroir law firm (known as Rose Law), and she ultimately decided to accept their offer and join the firm.

Hillary broke several barriers at Rose Law. She was the first female associate, and the presence of what some partners viewed as a "Yankee feminist" caused concern both among the male partners and the female secretarial staff, who criticized her casual dress and lack of makeup.

Hillary joined the litigation section and began working closely with attorneys Vince Foster and Webster Hubbell. She also continued her work on child advocacy, contributing a chapter to the book *Children's Rights: Contemporary Perspectives,* in which she argued that children had a right to live in a world at peace and to sue those industries (such as nuclear power plants) whose activities might negatively affect their future. In addition to her work for Rose Law, she handled several cases for children on a *pro bono* (free of charge) basis. Hillary was also quickly gaining an awareness of how Bill's career choices had placed both of them in the public eye. Bill Clinton had decided to run for governor of Arkansas, winning election in 1978. Hillary would remember the next two years as "the most difficult, exhilarating, glorious and heartbreaking in my life."[8]

Clinton had made dozens of campaign promises, and he quickly set to work trying to fulfill as many of them as possible. Within his first few days in office, he proposed bills to rebuild the state's highway system, reorganize public schools and build a network of health clinics in rural areas. Focus soon shifted from Clinton's overwhelming barrage of legislative proposals to his wife, and Hillary—the Yankee woman who had refused to take her husband's name—quickly became a lightning rod for critics, a role she would play throughout her husband's career. Citizens of Arkansas were used to governors' wives who were matronly, who had carefully sprayed and styled hair and wore pastel-colored dresses. The presence of a First Lady with thick glasses, no makeup, dressed in oversized sweaters and bell-bottom jeans, came as a shock.

In an interview in the *Arkansas Democrat,* Hillary gave a tour of the private quarters of the Governor's Mansion while explaining that the role of First Lady would not be her full-time job: "I need to maintain my interests and my commitments. I need my own identity, too."[9]

In 1979, Hillary became a partner at the Rose Law Firm. She was only 32 years old. She was still working with Marian Wright Edelman's Children's Defense Fund, commuting to Washington every few months, helping with the Rural Health Advisory Committee her husband had created, and hosting events at the Governor's Mansion.

WHITEWATER

It was in the early years of Bill Clinton's first term as governor that he and his wife became involved with a land development plan that would become known as Whitewater. Businessman Jim McDougal and his wife, Susan, had been friends of Bill Clinton's before his marriage, and McDougal was involved in business ventures with many prominent people in Arkansas. Just before Clinton became governor, Jim McDougal invited the Clintons to join him and his wife in a business venture to develop 230 acres on the south bank of the White River in North Arkansas for use as vacation home sites. The region was a popular one for vacation homes, and the Clintons agreed to invest.

By the time that the land was purchased and the proposed

area of development was surveyed, interest rates were rising. As lots at the Whitewater Development Company, Inc. (the partnership formed by the Clintons and McDougals) were put on the market, the demand for vacation homes was shrinking. The Clintons and McDougals held on to the land, building a model home and hoping that interest rates would go down. The McDougals were more actively involved in managing the project, and the Clintons, according to Hillary, held on to the land to avoid taking a huge loss. "From time to time, over the next several years, Jim asked us to write checks to help make interest payments or other contributions, and we never questioned his judgment," Hillary later noted. "We didn't realize that he was becoming involved in a raft of dubious business schemes."[10]

Another investment would prove equally problematic for Hillary in the future. Shortly after forming the partnership with the McDougals, Hillary opened a commodities trading account. She was advised by Jim Blair, the fiancé of a close friend. Within ten months of trading, she earned nearly $100,000 in profit, closing her account in July 1979. Her advisor, Jim Blair, and many others would lose fortunes. The substantial amount of her profit, and the timing of the ending of her trading, would draw questions in the future.

NEW MOTHER

The Clintons had spent Christmas of 1978 in London, and during the vacation, the couple heard the Joni Mitchell song "Chelsea Morning." They agreed that if they ever had a daughter, they would name her Chelsea.

Just before midnight, on February 27, 1980, Chelsea Victoria Clinton was born. Hillary had spent the past few weeks litigating a difficult child custody case, determined to prove to her fellow attorneys that, even pregnant, she could work as hard as anyone. She approached motherhood with the same thoroughness as she had every other challenge,

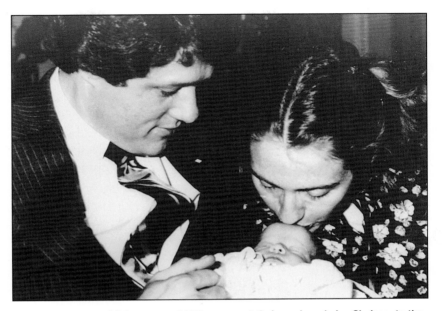

Bill, then governor of Arkansas, and Hillary present their newborn baby, Chelsea, to the public on March 5, 1980. Bill and Hillary met while they were studying law at Yale University and developed a relationship built on their mutual passion for Democratic politics. Despite the challenges of balancing her private and public roles, Hillary managed to both support Bill's career and establish her own.

reading pregnancy books and studying the latest theories on child development.

The reality of motherhood was not something that she could completely prepare for. On one of her first nights home from the hospital, Chelsea woke up crying inconsolably. The new parents tried everything to comfort her. Finally, Hillary looked down at her infant daughter. "Chelsea," she said, "this is new for both of us. I've never been a mother before, and you've never been a baby. We're just going to have to help each other do the best we can."[11]

Hillary was a fortunate new mother. Rose Law allowed her to take four months off from work to stay home with Chelsea. The Governor's Mansion provided her with additional resources—a cook, assistants, built-in babysitters, and a nanny.

Soon she was back to work, and the nation's youngest governor was running for reelection. Yet his reelection was not a sure thing. He had been ambitious, had surrounded himself with several advisors from out-of-state, and had instituted an unpopular increase in the cost of car tags—a small increase that made a big difference to many voters. Many voters still objected to the First Lady's decision to keep her maiden name, especially after the birth of her daughter. For Hillary, it was a logical decision—she was known professionally as Hillary Rodham—but to many voters it seemed suspicious.

The incumbent governor faced a Democratic opponent in the primary of 1980, a 78-year-old retired turkey farmer named Monroe Schwarzlose, who received one-third of the vote, thanks in part to a campaign that criticized the car tag increase and an administration that it claimed was "out of touch" with most people in Arkansas. Democratic president Jimmy Carter was struggling with economic woes and international crises (including the seizure of American hostages in Iran), and he created more problems for the Democratic governor who had supported him when he sent hundreds of detained Cuban refugees—many of them formerly inmates of mental hospitals or prisons—to a camp in Fort Chaffee, Arkansas. The detainees rioted in June, and Clinton was forced to send state troopers and the National Guard to maintain control of the camp. The problems increased when President Carter sent additional refugees to the Fort Chaffee camp only a few weeks after the riots.

Clinton's Republican opponent, Frank White, capitalized on the situation, suggesting that Clinton cared more about Jimmy Carter than Arkansas. The ads proved devastatingly effective, and Clinton lost the election.

A NEW APPROACH

After his term ended, the family moved to an older home in Little Rock, and Bill took a position with a Little Rock law firm and began to plan a new campaign, this time to win back the job of governor. Aides and colleagues relentlessly examined everything that had gone wrong in the first term that might have caused Clinton to lose the election and some of the attention shifted to his wife.

As Hillary ruefully noted, "People in Arkansas reacted to me much as my mother-in-law had when she first met me: I was an oddity because of my dress, my Northern ways and the use of my maiden name." [12] While Bill Clinton never pressured his wife to change her name, he was one of the few who did not. Finally, Hillary bowed to the pressure. "I decided," she said, "it was more important for Bill to be governor again than for me to keep my maiden name. So when Bill announced his run for another term on Chelsea's second birthday, I began calling myself Hillary Rodham Clinton." [13]

5

From the Governor's Mansion to the White House

1982–1992

Eleanor Roosevelt understood that every one of us every day has choices to make about the kind of person we are and what we wish to become. You can decide to be someone who brings people together, or you can fall prey to those who wish to divide us. You can be someone who educates yourself, or you can believe that being negative is clever and being cynical is fashionable. You have a choice.

—Hillary Rodham Clinton, *Living History*

It was more than a name change for the former governor's wife that helped Bill Clinton win back his spot in the Governor's Mansion. The 1982 election involved all of the Clintons, traveling around Arkansas, listening to the voters, stopping at small and large venues. Hillary, according to many, helped manage the campaign, helped develop some of its focus, and

Bill and Hillary celebrate Bill's win in the Democratic primary for governor of Arkansas on June 8, 1982. Bill and Hillary campaigned vigorously for his reelection; aside from reaching out to voters by making speeches, Hillary also revamped her image by lightening her hair, wearing contacts, and taking Bill's last name.

hired many of the experienced staff with whom they had worked on other campaigns.

Writer Gail Sheehy noted that Hillary's efforts on behalf

of her husband's campaign included a personal transformation that went beyond taking his name. She lightened her hair, began wearing contact lenses rather than her normal thick glasses, and subtly began to change her clothing choices as well.[1]

Both Clintons made it clear to Arkansans that they had listened to the voters, and that they had a better understanding of their expectations of their governor and his wife. In 1982, Clinton was elected governor with a new focus on education as one of his earliest mandates. In national surveys of state school systems, those in Arkansas consistently ranked among the worst in the nation. In his inaugural address, Clinton announced an initiative to change this problem, adding, "I have decided to name my wife, Hillary, as chairman of the cause. I think she'll have more time to exercise a sort of leadership and direction the commission needs."[2]

The plan for educational reform was a challenging one. Hillary traveled around Arkansas, observing first-hand the strengths and weaknesses of the state's school system. Her recommendations, presented in July 1983 at a joint state Senate–House legislative committee, were sweeping: mandatory full-day kindergarten, a student-to-teacher ratio no greater than 20 to 1, a stronger math and science curriculum, and testing students before they could be promoted. To bitter opposition from teacher's groups, she suggested teacher examinations and recommended continuing education for teachers.

The result of these recommendations—the steps needed to improve schools—would require a tax increase. Hillary's 90-minute presentation impressed the legislators. At the end, Representative Lloyd George called out, "Well, fellas, it looks like we might have elected the wrong Clinton!"[3]

Clinton easily won reelection in 1984 and 1986. By 1987, Democratic leaders were approaching him to consider a run for the presidency. He seriously debated it, but a number of personal factors influenced his ultimate decision that the time was not yet right: He was concerned about the impact of the campaign on seven-year-old Chelsea; his half-brother, Roger, had recently been released from prison for drug-related crimes; his mother was struggling with problems in her nursing practice; Hillary's father had suffered a stroke; and the Rodhams were in the process of moving to Little Rock.

It was a difficult decision, but Clinton continued as governor, winning reelection in 1988 and 1990. By 1991, with Chelsea now 11, Bill and Hillary again discussed the possibility of his seeking the presidency. Hillary summarized their decision as logical: "We figured: What did we have to lose? Even if Bill's run failed, he would have the satisfaction of knowing he had tried, not just to win, but to make a difference for America. That seemed to be a risk worth taking."[4]

THE CAMPAIGN TRAIL

On October 3, 1991, Bill Clinton stood in front of Little Rock's Old State House with Hillary and Chelsea by his side and announced his decision to run for president of the United States. Hillary was 44 years old, Bill was 46. They both had worked on previous presidential campaigns, but as Hillary noted:

> We were unprepared for the hardball politics and relentless scrutiny that comes with a run for the Presidency. Bill had to make the case nationwide for his political beliefs, and we had to endure exhaustive inspection of every aspect of our lives. We had to get acquainted with a national press corps that knew little about us and even less about where we came from. And we had to manage our own emotions in the glare of the public spotlight, through the course of an increasingly mean spirited and personal campaign."[5]

They quickly assembled a strong, experienced team of advisors and staff to assist with the campaign effort. James Carville, one of the key strategists in the campaign, remembers his first meeting with Hillary:

> Some people will run over you just because you are there; other people will run around you, and some will run over you if you're in the way. Hillary won't run you down for fun and she won't run into a ditch to avoid scratching your fender, but if you are blocking something that we need to get accomplished, you'll get run over in a hurry. . . . You could disagree with Mrs. Clinton and that was fine. In fact, sometimes in order to get recognized you had to scream and say some outlandish things. But if you're going to differ with Hillary, be prepared. Go in there with all your reasoning in order, don't just shoot your mouth off and figure it out later.[6]

Hillary assembled her own campaign staff, a different practice from other campaigns, where a single staff managed both the candidate and his wife. She was quickly buffeted by questions that focused on her marriage, on her husband's actions during the 1960s when his peers were being drafted into the Vietnam War, and on precisely what her own role would be should her husband be elected president.

During the primary in New Hampshire, Bill Clinton introduced Hillary to the audience, citing her work on children's issues and joking that perhaps a new Clinton campaign slogan should be developed: "Buy one, get one free."[7] The offhand remark was intended to underscore his admiration for his wife's accomplishments and to remind the audience of what both Clintons had accomplished in Arkansas while he was governor, but it was quickly reported by the media in less than flattering terms.

Throughout the presidential campaign, and indeed through-out her husband's eight years as president, Hillary Rodham Clinton would attract attention in a way no other First Lady had. She was a strong, intelligent, accomplished woman with a career separate from her husband's. She was direct, involved in public issues and unashamed of her own desire to contribute her ideas to the political process.

Both Bill and Hillary were forced to answer numerous questions about her role in a Clinton administration. They were asked whether or not she planned to serve as vice president ("I'm not interested in attending a lot of funerals around the world," she quickly replied), and when she told an audience in 1991, "We'll have a women president by 2010," she was asked whether or not she would be the candidate. "We'll talk later," Hillary responded.[8]

Questions about the strength of their marriage and accusations by a woman named Gennifer Flowers, who claimed to have had a long-term relationship with Bill Clinton, prompted Bill and Hillary to agree to an appearance on the news program *60 Minutes* in January 1992, which aired after the Super Bowl. The couple refused to answer detailed questions about any problems in their marriage, but when interviewer Steve Kroft referred to her marriage as an "arrangement," Hillary became angry.

"You know," she said, "I'm not sitting here—some little woman standing by my man like Tammy Wynette. I'm sitting here because I love him, and I honor what we've been through together. And you know, if that's not enough for people, then heck, don't vote for him."[9]

BAKING COOKIES

Hillary was not naïve; she had weathered several campaigns and knew that the media—and the voters who studied their coverage—would analyze her clothes, her hair, and certainly her words. Yet the stress of the constant scrutiny led to even the simplest comments becoming fodder for her critics. In March 1991, just before the important primaries in Illinois and Michigan, Hillary was at a lunch stop in Chicago when she was asked whether or not her legal practice had created a conflict of interest while her husband was governor of Arkansas. Hillary quickly replied, "I suppose I could have stayed home and baked cookies and had tea." [10]

The off-the-cuff comment was seized upon as evidence that Hillary had little respect for women who chose to stay at home and raise children. She was forced to learn a difficult lesson: Her chosen role in this campaign was quite different from that of other women whose husbands had run for president:

> While Bill talked about social change, I embodied it. I had my own opinions, interests and profession. For better or worse, I was outspoken. I represented a fundamental change in the way women functioned in our society. And if my husband won, I would be filling a position in which the duties were not spelled out, but the performance was judged by everybody. I was being labeled and categorized because of my positions and mistakes, and also because I had been turned into a symbol for women of my generation. [11]

Several years later, in her book *It Takes a Village,* Hillary referred to the "cookies-and-tea" comment and the criticism it sparked:

> Many people jumped to conclusions about me, both positive and negative, based as much on how they interpreted what I said as on the words themselves. Few heard my full comments or knew much about me before labeling me in one way or another. I learned important lessons from the whole episode, one of which is that when I am asked a question that relates to

me personally, I have to be aware that my answer may be measured by how people feel about the choices they've made in their own lives. But the incident also highlighted for me the amount of energy that is wasted on public and private sniping over women's and men's choices and on stereotyping their values, abilities, and predilections.[12]

In July 1992, the Democratic Party formally nominated Bill Clinton as its candidate for the presidency. The convention was held in New York City. Clinton had chosen Senator Al Gore from Tennessee as his running mate, breaking with the tradition of choosing a vice presidential candidate quite different from the presidential candidate to "balance the ticket." Clinton and Gore were both from southern states, were approximately the same age, and shared similar viewpoints on critical issues. Immediately after the convention, Bill and Hillary, and Al Gore and his wife, Tipper, set out on a tour of the country, traveling from one campaign spot to another by bus. The couples spent long days together getting off the bus at various points to chat with small or large crowds.

The campaign focused on the differences between incumbent President George H. W. Bush and Bill Clinton. Bush had enjoyed huge public support following the Gulf War, but in the period between its end and the election, the economy had suffered. Unemployment was high, interest rates were high, healthcare costs were high. Clinton and Gore's energetic approach to campaigning emphasized their youth and their plan for a "new direction." President Bush frequently seemed out of touch, expressing surprise at prices in a supermarket during one appearance and seeming puzzled by the technology of a checkout scanner.

During the final 24 hours of the campaign, Bill and Hillary crisscrossed the country, stopping in Philadelphia, Cleveland,

Detroit, St. Louis, and Albuquerque. They campaigned in Texas, Kentucky, and Colorado before traveling back early on the morning of election day to cast their votes in Little Rock. They

INAUGURAL ADDRESS

On Wednesday, January 21, 1993, William Jefferson Clinton became the 42nd president of the United States. In his First Inaugural Address, he emphasized that a new generation was coming to power, one that was assuming responsibilities for governing in a different world from that of previous generations:

Today we celebrate the mystery of American renewal. This ceremony is held in the depth of winter. But, by the words we speak and the faces we show the world, we force the spring. . . . A spring reborn in the world's oldest democracy that brings forth the vision and courage to reinvent America.

When our founders boldly declared America's independence to the world and our purposes to the Almighty, they knew that America, to endure, would have to change. Not change for change's sake, but change to preserve America's ideals—life, liberty, the pursuit of happiness. Though we march to the music of our time, our mission is timeless.

Each generation of Americans must define what it means to be American. . . . Our democracy must be not only the envy of the world but the engine of our own renewal. There is nothing wrong with America that cannot be cured by what is right with America . . .

In serving, we recognize a simple but powerful truth—we need each other. And we must care for one another. Today, we do more than celebrate America; we rededicate ourselves to the very idea of America.*

* Bill Clinton, "First Inaugural Address," January 21, 1993.
  http://bartleby.com/124/pres64/html

spent the day at the Governor's Mansion. Before 11:00 P.M., the networks announced that Bill Clinton would become the next president of the United States.

Gail Sheehy, in her biography of Hillary Clinton, recounted a joke that reflected the popular perception of the importance Hillary played in her husband's rise to the presidency. In the story, President Clinton and the First Lady were out driving in the country near Hillary's hometown. The presidential limousine pulled into a gas station, where an attendant appeared and offered to fill up the gas tank. He then recognized the First Lady and said, "Hey, Hillary, remember me? We used to date in high school."

After chatting for a few minutes, the Clintons' limousine drove off, and Bill smugly said to Hillary, "You used to date that guy? Just think what it would be like if you had married him." Hillary shrugged and replied, "If I'd married him, you'd be pumping gas, and he'd be president."[13]

MOVING TO THE WHITE HOUSE

In addition to the many details necessary to establishing a transition team and preparing for the presidency, the Clintons had to pack up their belongings and prepare for a move to the White House, and they needed to find a new school in Washington for Chelsea. Hillary also needed to focus on her role as First Lady—what she would do with the opportunities and responsibilities the role provided.

Hillary studied the contributions previous First Ladies had made, taking as her role models several that she felt were the most effective. One of these was Eleanor Roosevelt, who described the struggle to remember that she was not just "Eleanor Roosevelt," but the "wife of the president." "I was only a symbol," Roosevelt noted in her autobiography, *This I Remember*, "as wives of presidents had always been and would always be."[14] Hillary wanted to be more than a symbol; she wanted to be a political partner.

Early on, Clinton decided that economic and healthcare policy would be the two focuses of his early days in office. A structure to handle economic policy was quickly set up; for healthcare, Clinton decided that he wanted Hillary to lead the initiative, to help transform the administration's proposals into legislation. Hillary had led committees on rural healthcare and education while Bill was governor; to both Hillary and Bill, this seemed like a logical extension of her background and skills.

Hillary had taken a leave of absence from her law practice during the campaign. Once Bill won the election, she resigned her position and began to assemble her staff.

The task Hillary had undertaken—to reform the American healthcare system—was massive and complicated. The health-care sector represented one-seventh of the American economy, and the position demonstrated the important role Hillary would play in the administration—a role more prominent than that of previous First Ladies. President Clinton had promised to deliver a comprehensive healthcare package in his administration's first 100 days, a deadline he added to an already controversial plan.

Hillary's first move was a symbolic one. First Ladies had traditionally had their offices in the East Wing of the White House, a wing that housed office space, a reception room, and the White House movie theater. The real business of the presidency was carried out in the West Wing. The West Wing contained the Oval Office, the Roosevelt Room, the Cabinet Room, the Situation Room, the White House Mess (where meals are served), and the offices of the president's senior staff. In a break with tradition, Hillary was given an office on the second floor of the West Wing, down the hall from the domestic policy staff. Her own staff was integrated into the president's staff, and her assistant attended meetings with the president's senior staff.

In addition to broadening the role of a First Lady, Hillary could not ignore the traditional responsibilities of the president's wife. She was required to host White House dinners, working closely with her social secretary to select the ideal combination of linens and place settings, the best seating arrangements, the correct flowers, and theme for formal events.

Early on, Hillary met with former First Lady Jacqueline Kennedy Onassis, who offered the benefit of her own experience raising two children in the White House and who had gained a reputation for infusing the role of First Lady with style and glamour. Onassis, who had been only 31 when her husband was elected president, stressed the importance of providing Chelsea with as normal a life as possible while trying to shield her from the press. She urged Hillary to go to Camp David and stay with friends whenever possible to retreat from the stress of life in the White House. Concerned about the criticism over her fashion sense, Hillary shared with Onassis her idea of simply turning herself over to a team of consultants for a fashion makeover. "You have to be you," replied a horrified Onassis. "You'll end up wearing someone else's idea of who you are and how you should look. Concentrate instead on what's important to you." [15]

Inspired by Jacqueline Kennedy Onassis' example, Hillary determined to gradually put her own stamp on her new home. The White House cuisine, under Kennedy and successive presidents, had been French in flavor and style; Hillary decided to reintroduce American cuisine to the White House menu. The new emphasis on fresh, American ingredients and American wines was, to Hillary, a logical extension of her traditional responsibilities as First Lady, but once more it sparked criticism. To some critics, it seemed impossible that she could head up the committee studying healthcare reform and also oversee place settings and menus.

Several years later, speaking in Beijing at the United Nations Fourth World Conference on Women, Hillary spoke passionately about her right—and the rights of all women—

to create their own balance between their professional and personal roles:

> We need to understand that there is no formula for how women should lead their lives. That is why we must respect the choices that each woman makes for herself and her family. Every woman deserves the chance to realize her God-given potential.[16]

A NEW CHALLENGE

Hillary immersed herself in the details of the healthcare debate. She worked closely with business consultant Ira Magaziner, who had produced an important study on healthcare costs. Hillary was assigned to chair the task force studying healthcare; Magaziner was responsible for managing the day-to-day operations as senior advisor for policy and planning.

Early on, both Hillary and Magaziner were concerned that the president's self-imposed deadline of 100 days for delivering a healthcare reform bill to Congress was unrealistic. Previous administrations had attempted to reform the national healthcare system—including Presidents Franklin Roosevelt with a national health insurance system, Harry Truman with universal healthcare coverage, and Lyndon Johnson with the creation of Medicaid and Medicare. More recent presidents, including Nixon, Ford, and Carter, had all attempted and failed to reform the healthcare system.

Hillary believed passionately in the issue of providing healthcare to the millions of uninsured Americans, who had no access to healthcare until a medical crisis arose, when they were forced to seek the most expensive kind of treatment—emergency room care. Rising healthcare costs forced more and more small businesses to stop offering health insurance to their workers. Doctors were forced to operate under increasing restrictions on the kind of care they could provide, and health insurance providers frequently opposed any program offering universal coverage.

On January 25, 1992, before an audience of senior staff and journalists, Bill Clinton announced that Hillary would chair the newly formed President's Task Force on National Healthcare Reform, which would include the secretaries of Health and Human Services, Treasury, Defense, Commerce and Labor, as well as the directors of Veterans Affairs and of the Office of Management and Budget and senior White House Staff. "We're going to have to make some tough choices in order to control healthcare costs and to provide healthcare for all," President Clinton said. "I am grateful that Hillary has agreed to chair the taskforce, and not only because it means she'll be sharing some of the heat I expect to generate." [17]

6

The Healthcare Debate
1992–1994

What did you do to make your husband so mad at you . . . He'd have to be awfully upset about something to put you in charge of such a thankless task [as health care reform].
—Governor Mario Cuomo of New York, quoted in *Living History*

Eleanor Roosevelt, one of the First Ladies Hillary most admired, once explained that her influence over her husband was far less than many people imagined:

> I never tried to exert any political influence on my husband or on anyone else in the government. However, one cannot live in a political atmosphere and study the actions of a good politician, which my husband was, without absorbing some rudimentary facts about politics. From him I learned that a good politician is marked to a

great extent by his sense of timing. He says the right thing at the right moment. Though the immediate reaction may be unfavorable, in the long run it turns out that what he said needed to be said at the time he said it." [1]

As the Clinton administration began its first hundred days, few could argue that the American system of healthcare was not desperately in need of reform. Still, the timing did come under question. The administration was under intense pressure in the early days. Key appointments needed to be filled. Staffs needed to be organized. An economic plan was a priority.

Hillary was not deterred. Clinton administration senior advisor George Stephanopoulos recalled the First Lady studying briefing books and polls, presiding at public hearings, wooing senators and representatives, and ultimately traveling across the country to share the administration's vision of preventive care, cost control, and a consistent system of national care. The program, Stephanopoulos noted, was designed to "save lives and prove to the world that a first lady could be a fully public presidential partner." [2]

Concerned by the frequent leaks of information coming from the White House, Hillary decided to set up her own independent staff to work on healthcare reform, a staff that reported directly to Hillary, had its own center of operations and schedule, and was dubbed "the Intensive Care Unit." The staff, and the meetings related to healthcare, were conducted behind closed doors in an effort to stem the flow of leaks before the proposals had been finalized. The result of many of these meetings was a charge that the White House was operating "in secret," and questions began to build about precisely to what extent the healthcare system would be altered by the new plans.

As Hillary noted, "Our goals were simple enough: We wanted a plan that dealt with all aspects of the healthcare system rather than one that tinkered on the margins. We wanted a process that considered a variety of ideas and allowed for healthy discussion and debate. And we wanted to adhere to congressional wishes as much as we could. Almost immediately, we hit turbulence."[3]

Ira Magaziner had organized a team of "experts" to advise the President's Task Force on the various aspects of healthcare. Nearly 600 people made up this team, including representatives from the various government agencies, congressional offices, healthcare representatives, doctors, nurses, hospital administrators, even economists. Needless to say, this large group quickly became unwieldy, presenting wide-ranging viewpoints and clashing on nearly every policy point. The Association of American Physicians and Surgeons sued the task force, claiming that because Hillary was not a government employee, she should not be allowed to chair or even attend closed task force meetings. Their argument was that any meeting chaired by a non–government employee should be open to outsiders, including the media.

Soon, Hillary witnessed firsthand the realities of devastating illness on patients and their family members. On March 19, only two months after moving into the White House, Hillary received word that her father had suffered a massive stroke. Hillary quickly returned to Little Rock, accompanied by her brother Tony and Chelsea. There she discovered that 82-year-old Hugh Rodham had slipped into a coma.

For days, Hillary, her brothers, her mother, and Chelsea took turns sitting next to Hugh Rodham's hospital bed, talking, singing, telling family stories, listening to sounds of the machinery in his hospital room, hoping for some slight indication that he was aware that they were there. Bill, his mother, her new husband, Dick Kelley, and other friends arrived and spent time with the family. Hillary would later learn that Virginia Kelley had arrived in Little Rock after undergoing treatment for cancer, which had only recently been diagnosed.

For Hillary, the importance of her work in Washington faded. By March 28, it was clear that her father was brain dead and being kept alive only by technology. The family gathered, and all agreed that Hugh Rodham would not want to spend the rest of his life in this condition. They agreed to take him off the respirator and then said their good-byes.

Hugh Rodham, however, did not die within 24 hours as his doctors had predicted. Instead, he began to breathe on his own, remaining in a coma. The family struggled with the prospect of needing to insert a feeding tube and moving Hugh to a nursing home. Hillary was finally forced to return to the White House on April 4 so that Chelsea could resume school and so that she could return to some of her regular duties as First Lady.

On April 6, Hillary flew to Austin, Texas, to speak as part of a lecture series organized by Liz Carpenter, the press secretary of former President Lyndon Johnson's wife, Lady Bird Johnson. Before an audience at the University of Texas in Austin, she delivered a speech that talked of a "spiritual vacuum," reflecting her emotions over her father's illness and the implications her new awareness had for healthcare reform:

> We need a new politics of meaning. We need a new ethos of individual responsibility and caring. We need a new definition of civil society which answers the unanswerable questions posed by both the market forces and the governmental ones, as to how we can have a society that fills us up again and makes us feel that we are part of something bigger than ourselves.[4]

The speech would be criticized in the *New York Times Magazine*, which would mock the First Lady as "Saint Hillary" in an article published a few weeks after the speech.

The day after the speech, Hugh Rodham died.

TRAVELGATE

The 100-day deadline for passage of a healthcare reform package came and went. The majority of the White House staff,

THE GREAT SOCIETY

Bill Clinton was not the first president to attempt a sweeping program of healthcare reform. Many of his predecessors had introduced legislation, but one of the most successful programs was developed by Lyndon Johnson, who in 1964 introduced his vision of a "Great Society"—an America where there would be no poverty and no racial injustice, where education would be available to all, where the elderly would receive the care they needed, and where the nation's natural resources would be protected.

Johnson won a landslide victory in the presidential election of 1964; his party (Democrats) formed two-thirds of the majority in both the House and Senate. With these victories, Johnson introduced many sweeping legislative proposals, including programs to provide healthcare to the poor and elderly, known as Medicaid and Medicare.

"No longer will older Americans be denied the healing miracle of modern medicine," Johnson said on July 30, 1965, when he signed the Medicare bill into law. "No longer will illness crush and destroy the savings they have so carefully put away over a lifetime so that they might enjoy dignity in their later years."*

Medicare—an amendment to President Franklin Roosevelt's 1935 Social Security Act—was designed to provide supplementary health insurance and hospital insurance for all Americans age 65 and older. On that same day, Johnson signed into law Medicaid—also an amendment to Social Security—which was designed to provide national health insurance for low-income Americans.

As the American population ages and the number of Americans eligible for Medicare grows, the viability of this critical component of President Johnson's "Great Society" program has been called into question.

* Lyndon B. Johnson, "Medicare Speech," July 30, 1965.
  http://www.historychannel.com/speeches/archive/speech_147.html

including the president, was focused on the economy, shaping a new budget, and developing economic policy. Opposition to the proposals that had been leaked from the Task Force was building, and some Democratic representatives were proposing their own healthcare plans.

To further complicate the situation, the plan for universal coverage was expanding to include new elements. Many of these were proposed by Hillary herself. Dental care for children, psychiatric care, drug and alcohol recovery programs, and long-term nursing home care were all added to the coverage deemed vital.

While wrestling with the healthcare package, Hillary found herself immersed in a crisis involving the White House Travel Office. Told by her close friend, former Rose Law partner, and assistant White House counsel Vince Foster that a discrepancy had been uncovered in the finances of the White House Travel Office, Hillary told Foster to take care of it.

Foster ordered an emergency audit and discovered that approximately $18,000 in funds was missing or unaccounted for and other instances of financial mismanagement and waste were uncovered. The FBI was called in to investigate—a mistake in hindsight, because the situation should have been turned over to the attorney general to investigate. In addition, the head of the White House Travel Office, Billy Dale (who had served in the position for 32 years), and his staff were dismissed without being given a chance to provide explanations for the financial irregularities.

The White House Travel Office is responsible for, among other things, arranging travel and accommodations for the group of reporters who travel with the president. It was clearly unwise to summarily dismiss a group that had such close media ties without being certain that the charges were justified and that proper procedures had been followed. To make matters worse, employees of WorldWide Travel, an agency whose head was a distant cousin of Bill

Clinton, was put in charge of the Travel Office following the dismissals.

The press coverage that followed was harshly critical, both of the actions and of the possible involvement of Hillary in the firings. Chief of Staff Mack McLarty was forced to rescind the firings of five of the travel office employees who had no connection to financial accounting and to remove the WorldWide employees who had assumed positions in the travel office.

The implications of what the media dubbed "Travelgate" would continue, despite the changes made by McLarty. Dale and other members of the White House Travel Office staff would be investigated by the FBI. Hillary's role in the firings would draw questions, and precisely what her instructions were—and to whom—would become a subject of inquiry. Finally, Vince Foster would also draw criticism for his role in the firings and for the legal advice he was providing. The *Wall Street Journal* was particularly harsh in its treatment of Foster.

Foster was under intense pressure, working long hours to research medical malpractice law for the healthcare task force and providing legal advice on the details involving the records of the Whitewater Development Company, whose financial improprieties had drawn their own criticism. Not accustomed to the scrutiny and press criticism that accompanied politics, Foster sank into depression.

On July 20, while Hillary was in Little Rock visiting her mother with Chelsea, she received a phone call from Mack McLarty informing her that Vince Foster's body had been discovered in a park, apparently the result of suicide. Hillary was devastated and horrified. The suicide would trigger endless conspiracy theories, speculating about the extent of her relationship with Foster, about whether or not he had been murdered, and concerning critical files relating to Hillary and Whitewater that were removed from Foster's office after his death.

In a six-month period, Hillary had seen her husband become president of the United States, had suffered the deaths of both her father and a close friend, had learned that her mother-in-law was dying from cancer, and had suffered intense personal and professional criticism. "I'm sure that I sometimes appeared brittle, sad and even angry—because I was," Hillary remembered. "I knew that I had to carry on and bear the pain I felt in private. This was one of the times when I kept going on sheer willpower."

HEALTHCARE DECISIONS

The Clinton administration passed its budget plan in late August, and, after a brief vacation in Martha's Vineyard with her husband, Hillary returned to Washington determined to focus on healthcare. The president scheduled a speech before Congress on September 22 to discuss the healthcare plan, and Hillary and her team determined that prior to the address it was critical to discuss the plan's contents with certain key Democratic representatives to help ensure their support.

The plan was still in its raw stages, with many of the figures being revised, when Democratic staffers were invited to review the draft document. Immediately, the contents of the draft began leaking out, sparking debate before the plan had even been finalized. The Health Insurance Association of America launched a series of television advertisements critical of the reform plan, in which an older couple—"Harry" and "Louise"—sat at a kitchen table worrying that the new healthcare plan would mean changes they didn't want.

On September 22, 1993, Bill Clinton appeared before a joint session of Congress to announce the launch of the healthcare plan. Hillary sat in the balcony accompanied by famed pediatrician and author Dr. T. Berry Brazelton and President Reagan's surgeon general, Dr. C. Everett Koop. Clinton began to speak, honoring Hillary with the acknowledgement that the plan required a "talented navigator—someone with a rigorous mind, a steady compass, a caring heart. Luckily for me and our nation, I didn't have to look

Hillary listens appreciatively to President Clinton's speech to a joint session of Congress on September 22, 1993, announcing the launch of the healthcare plan she had developed. Despite Hillary's tireless efforts to rally support for the healthcare package, her plan was never passed. Hillary was greatly criticized for the proposal, which was considered too inflexible and complex to serve the public's best interest.

very far."[6] What the audience did not realize was that the wrong speech had been loaded into the Teleprompter, and for seven minutes the president delivered his address from memory while aides frantically scrambled behind the scenes to load the correct speech into the machine and scroll quickly through the text until they had caught up with the president.

A week later, Hillary was invited to speak before senators and representatives to present the plan. She testified and answered questions for two hours, leaving the congressmen impressed by her poise and the depth of her knowledge.

Other First Ladies had testified before Congress, but Hillary's September 28 appearance marked the first time that a First Lady was a lead witness in a major administration legislative initiative.

"During the past months, as I have worked to educate myself about the problems facing our nation and facing American citizens about healthcare, I have learned a great deal," Hillary told the congressional committee. "The official reason I am here today is because I have had that responsibility. But more importantly for me, I'm here as a mother, a wife, a daughter, a sister, a woman. I'm here as an American citizen concerned about the health of her family and the health of her nation."[7]

For the next two days, Hillary appeared before House and Senate committees, speaking publicly about the plan that she had worked on for so long. Initially, the president had planned to take the new program on the road, holding town meetings and giving speeches around the country to generate support for healthcare reform. Yet a series of international events— attacks on American forces in Somalia and a planned coup of Russian President Boris Yeltsin—made healthcare less of a priority for the administration.

The original plan had been to present Congress with an outline of points that would form the healthcare legislation. Congress, however, did not want an outline; it wanted a detailed bill. The attempts to draft a detailed bill resulted in numerous groups insisting that specific points be included that most likely should have been edited out. Details about the number of childhood vaccinations and well-child visits deemed necessary, about nursing home facilities, even about the ideal racial composition of medical school classes, were all included in the final proposal submitted to Congress. The proposal weighed in at an overwhelming 1,342 pages when it was finally delivered by the White House to Congress on October 27.

A few weeks later, the bill was introduced by Senate Majority Leader George Mitchell. The length of the bill immediately drew criticism and even ridicule. Hillary refused to consider attempts to streamline the bill or agree to compromise legislation proposed by other congressmen. Clinton senior advisor George Stephanopolous later theorized that Hillary might not have been the best person to head the healthcare reform initiative:

> By choosing his wife to head the effort, we believed, Clinton was showing how much he cared about healthcare, and Hillary had all the right tools. She knew the subject cold, she was a tough-minded political tactician who could organize a national campaign, and her public advocacy was brilliant. Yet the approach she developed reflected both her strengths and her weaknesses. The plan, like the woman who guided it, was ambitious, idealistic and highly logical; but it was also inflexible, overly complex, and highly susceptible to misinterpretation. [8]

HEALTH SECURITY EXPRESS

The debate over healthcare reform would continue for nearly a year. Hillary traveled across the country, passionately speaking out on behalf of the healthcare bill. By the summer of 1994, inspired by the example of the Freedom Riders, who had preached a message in support of desegregation by traveling across the South in buses, and by the Clinton–Gore successful bus campaign, Hillary and her aides had organized their own bus tour. Known as the "Health Security Express," the bus crisscrossed the country advocating the policies of the health reform package. The hope was to inspire grassroots support for healthcare reform, sending a message to Congress to pass the package.

By then, the opposition to the bill had grown more organized. In taking such a public role in her husband's administration,

Hillary had crossed a barrier, a barrier that had precluded other First Ladies from drawing the fiercest criticism. By arguing that she had a role to play in the Clinton administration, that she was both qualified and justified in advising her husband on matters of domestic policy, Hillary had also made it more acceptable for criticism by opponents to the plan to be directed not only at the president but at his wife, as well.

Writer Gail Sheehy noted that Hillary was "the lightning rod for people's fear of change: the change of generation, the change of political leadership, the change in the equation between men and women, the tremendous social dislocation brought about by moving into a new information-based economy."[9] At the time of the Clinton administration, talk radio programs hosted by supporters of conservative policies—people like Rush Limbaugh and G. Gordon Liddy, among others—were enjoying huge audiences. Limbaugh, Liddy, and others wasted no time in depicting Hillary as a power-hungry feminist, urging their listeners to greet the Health Security Express with jeers and heckling.

At a speech in Seattle, the Secret Service was so concerned about the type of audience gathering for the healthcare speeches—including militia supporters, tax protestors, and antiabortion activists—that they urged Hillary to wear a bulletproof vest. She reluctantly agreed, believing that her opponents had become so strident that she faced real danger. Her words in Seattle were greeted with boos and heckling so loud that at times she could barely hear her own voice. Pulling away from the site of the speech, her limousine was surrounded by hundreds of protestors who screamed their disapproval. Later, Hillary learned that the Secret Service had arrested several of the protestors, confiscating a knife and two guns.

Hillary's opponents went beyond right-wing radio hosts and their audience. With mid-term elections nearing, her husband's Republican opponents had discovered that, by attacking healthcare reform—and Hillary—they could successfully weaken the reelection campaigns of Democrats. They had little interest in supporting a sweeping healthcare proposal introduced by a Democratic president.

Some Congressmen attempted to work out bipartisan support for the bill, or present an alternate version of the bill. Hillary had hoped that the president would speak out forcefully in support of the bill, pointing out to the nation the ways in which his Republican opponents had worked to derail the bill. Clinton took a more cautious approach.

After 20 months of effort, Hillary was forced to concede defeat. Congress adjourned on August 26, 1994, without acting on the Clinton healthcare plan, and Senate Majority Leader George Mitchell made an announcement that comprehensive, universal health insurance would not pass the Congress that year. The bill failed in its most basic goal: to persuade Americans with health insurance that reform would still guarantee them the same basic benefits and choice. It was a bitter disappointment to Hillary. Never again would she take such a visible, public policy role in her husband's administration.

Scandals and Hope
1994–1998

> I'm sick and tired of people who say that if you debate and
> disagree with this administration, somehow you're not patriotic.
> We need to stand up and say we're Americans, and we have
> the right to debate and disagree with any administration.
> —Hillary Rodham Clinton, *Living History*

As the healthcare reform bill was withering, Hillary faced even
more criticism and questions, this time for a failed investment
from many years earlier. Questions about the Whitewater land
development plan in which she and Bill had invested in
Arkansas began to pop up with greater frequency.

It began on Halloween 1993, with an article in the *Washington
Post* noting that an investigation was being launched into
Madison Guaranty Savings and Loan, owned by the Clintons'
partners in the Whitewater Development Company, Jim and

Susan McDougal. As the investigation proceeded, it was revealed that Jim McDougal, whose behavior had become increasingly irrational in recent years, was guilty of serious financial improprieties. He had opened Madison Guaranty, a small savings-and-loan, in 1982 and began a series of investments. When he was unable to cover the payments on his investments, he shifted money from one source to another, in one instance using Whitewater Development Company to buy property south of Little Rock for development, property that he named Castle Grande Estates.

The Clintons had been unaware of the majority of McDougal's other clients or investments until 1986 when Hillary became concerned by McDougal's refusal to take the Clintons' name off the Whitewater mortgage, despite his request for the Clintons to sign over their 50 percent share in the company. Up until then, Hillary had viewed Whitewater as simply a failed investment, but McDougal's hesitation to produce the bookkeeping records upon her request alarmed her. Hillary later explained that, at this point, she discovered that McDougal had not submitted corporate tax returns or paid property taxes on Whitewater. It took several years for Hillary to work through the back taxes, uncover the paperwork, and extricate her and her husband from a failed investment.

McDougal quickly went from a Clinton supporter to an enemy. In 1990, he checked himself into a psychiatric hospital shortly before facing trial for conspiracy, fraud, false statements, and fiscal misdealing. He soon linked up with critics of the Clintons, creating a controversy over the land operation and linking their names with his own multifaceted financial improprieties.

The scandal had surfaced earlier, during the election, and at that time the Clintons had hired attorneys and accountants to prepare detailed reports on the full facts of Whitewater, including the evidence that they had lost some $46,000 on their investment. As the rumors again began to swirl in 1994, the

Clintons once again hired an attorney, David Kendall, to put together a brief in response to questions from the *Washington Post* and other sources.

Hillary, Bill, and their advisors debated the best way to handle these questions. Should they produce the documents they had related to the Whitewater investment? If so, which ones? Should they answer all questions, some of the questions, or simply refer to the earlier investigation and its result? Their advisors split into two camps—those who argued that any and all paperwork related to Whitewater should be produced and, in fact, "dumped" on the media to demonstrate that there was nothing to hide, and those (chiefly the lawyers) who believed that releasing the documents was a slippery slope, because they did not know the full extent of McDougal's business dealings and might still give the appearance of holding back facts. Hillary sided with this view, and in the end the Clintons decided to make it clear that they would provide government investigators with any documents they needed but would not release paperwork to the media.

INDEPENDENT COUNSEL

On January 6, 1994, Hillary and Bill learned that Virginia Kelley had died in her sleep in Hot Springs. As the president mourned his mother's death, Republicans began issuing a call for an independent counsel to investigate the Whitewater deal. Some on Clinton's staff felt that it was better to simply agree to an independent counsel, arguing that one would probably be forced on the White House and because there was nothing to the so-called "scandal," it was better to get the investigation over with, but Hillary differed:

> My gut instinct, as a lawyer and a veteran of the Watergate impeachment inquiry staff, was to cooperate fully with any legitimate criminal inquiry but to resist giving someone free rein to probe indiscriminately and

indefinitely. A "special" investigation should be triggered only by credible evidence of wrongdoing, and there was no such evidence. Without credible evidence, a call for a special prosecutor would set a terrible precedent: From then on, every unsubstantiated charge against a president concerning events during any period of his life could require a special prosecutor.[1]

Finally, reluctantly, the president decided to ask Attorney General Janet Reno to appoint a special prosecutor, hoping that the investigation would be handled speedily and clear up any remaining questions about Whitewater. By January 20, 1994, Republican Robert Fiske had been appointed to serve as special prosecutor. Fiske had extensive prosecutorial experience and enjoyed a reputation for being thorough and fair. He took a leave of absence from his Wall Street law firm and began his investigation.

AN OLD FRIEND

In mid-March 1994, Webster Hubbell, Hillary's former partner and friend at Rose Law, announced his decision to resign from the Justice Department. The media had been reporting rumors of questionable billing practices while Hubbell was with Rose Law, including padding his expenses and overcharging clients. Hillary assumed that Hubbell was simply being victimized by untrue rumors, but she understood his wish to resign to avoid prolonging the story. He would be indicted only a few months later.

Questions about Hillary's involvement in Whitewater, her commodities trading and the profit she made, and her involvement with Webster Hubbell soon dominated the news. She held a press conference attempting to answer some of the questions.

Then in May 1994, more bad news arrived. A woman named Paula Jones filed a civil suit against Bill Clinton, accusing him of sexual harassment while he was governor.

Hillary speaks to the press on April 22, 1994 to address the numerous questions concerning her and President Clinton's responsibility in the Travelgate, Webster Hubbell, and Whitewater scandals. Despite Hillary's attempts to return attention to healthcare reform, a string of accusations regarding President Clinton's sexual impropriety with other women began to emerge soon after Hillary's press conference.

As Hillary traveled across the country, attempting to garner support for the healthcare bill, Robert Fiske announced his preliminary findings in the Whitewater investigation, which served to clarify the Clintons' role and made it clear that he had not uncovered any serious instances of wrongdoing.

On August 5, a new independent counsel was appointed to replace Fiske. Kenneth Starr, a 48-year-old Republican, was a choice that troubled the Clintons, because of his connection to more conservative allies and his lack of prosecutorial experience, as well as for his previous outspoken position in support of the Paula Jones lawsuit.

Although Bill Clinton was not on the ballot in the 1994 midterm elections, his policies and administration certainly were. Many viewed the sweeping success of Republican candidates in 1994 as evidence that voters had lost patience with Clinton and his program. The scandals that obscured his policies, the failure of healthcare reform, early missteps in political appointments and programs, all had weakened his administration.

On December 6, 1994, Kenneth Starr's office announced that Webster Hubbell was pleading guilty to mail fraud and tax evasion. Hubbell had confessed to cheating his clients and partners at Rose Law of nearly $400,000 by submitting false bills to cover his own personal expenses for some three years. It was a devastating blow to Hillary. Her two closest friends at Rose Law—Vince Foster and Webster Hubbell—had both been irreparably damaged by her husband's presence in the White House. Foster had committed suicide; now Hubbell faced prison.

THE LANGUAGE OF SILENCE

As the investigations into her legal practice and investments continued, Hillary focused on those areas where she believed she could make a difference. She researched the controversial health issue known as "Gulf War Syndrome," in which men and women who had served in the military in the Persian Gulf during Operation Desert Storm in 1991 reported chronic fatigue, gastrointestinal disorders, mysterious rashes, and respiratory problems. Hillary spoke with doctors and officials from the Department of Veterans Affairs and the Defense

Department. She persuaded her husband to appoint a task force to study the issue, although she was not appointed to serve on the committee. She championed the issue of mammograms, publicly encouraging older women to undergo the procedure.

Hillary also began to speak out in support of women's rights. She traveled outside the United States, speaking to a United Nations World Summit, then, accompanied by Chelsea, traveled to India, Pakistan, Nepal, Bangladesh, and Sri Lanka. It was a happy time for Hillary, a welcome escape from the scandals of Washington and a chance to ride elephants, to see the Taj Mahal, to spend time with her daughter, and to serve as an example of what women could accomplish.

Speaking before an audience in India, Hillary quoted the language of a poem written by a girl from New Delhi: "Too many women in too many countries speak the same language— of silence," she said.[2] Hillary used the moving speech as a springboard for her own theme: that issues affecting women should not be marginalized but should become a fundamental part of domestic and foreign policy decisions.

In 1995, Hillary also decided to focus more on her writing. She began penning a weekly newspaper column and also began to compile her thoughts on education and childrearing in a book that became *It Takes a Village*. The title was taken from the African proverb "It takes a village to raise a child," expressing Hillary's ideas that the responsibility for ensuring a safe, healthy and happy world for children extends beyond the family to encompass businesses and society.

In *It Takes a Village*, Hillary noted, "We cannot move forward by looking to the past for easy solutions. Even if a golden age had existed, we could not simply graft it onto today's busier, more impersonal and complicated world. Instead, our challenge is to arrive at a consensus of values and a common vision of what we can do today, individually and collectively, to build strong families and communities."[3]

Published in 1996, the book became a bestseller. Hillary donated the profits of the book to charity. Her audiotaped version of the book would earn her a Grammy Award.

SPEAKING OUT

As Hillary revised her ideas for *It Takes a Village*, she was invited to speak at the United Nations Fourth World Conference on Women. The conference was to be held in Beijing, China, in September 1995, and it would be the largest UN gathering in history. Hillary decided to accept the invitation, despite concerns over China's poor record on human rights.

It was an important opportunity to advance the cause of women—to speak out in support of women's rights to education, to healthcare, to greater opportunities. Delivering her remarks before a large audience at the plenary session, Hillary described the meeting as a "celebration of the contributions women make," explaining that the meeting's goals were to focus world attention "on issues that matter most in the lives of women and their families: access to education, healthcare, jobs and credit, the chance to enjoy basic legal and human rights and participate fully in the political life of their countries."[4] She stirred the delegates with her poise and passion, noting, "If there is one message that echoes forth from this conference, it is that human rights are women's rights—and women's rights are human rights."[5]

In Beijing, Hillary began to assume a new stature on the world stage. As a spokesperson for women's rights, she sparked tremendous pressure to create a climate of change in many countries where women had traditionally been subjugated. She soon added a new dimension to foreign policy by focusing on the plight of women refugees, women's access to credit, women's victimization in Bosnia, women's contributions to peace efforts in Ireland and Israel.

While on a book tour promoting *It Takes A Village*, Hillary learned that she would be subpoenaed to testify before a grand jury called by Kenneth Starr. Copies of Hillary's billing records from her time at Rose Law had been discovered in the White House; Starr wanted her to testify about the records.

Hillary was determined not to let her embarrassment at being summoned in such a public way show. She refused to take a secret entrance into the courthouse, stepping instead from a car in front of the U.S. District Court on January 26, 1996, smiling and waving to the crowd. She testified for four hours, then briefly answered questions before returning to the White House.

Hillary held her head high, as she had promised, and continued with her book tour. Later, she would ask reporters, "Why does this keep happening to me? Why are people dogging me like this? What's wrong here?" A reporter replied that the public didn't see the Hillary White House reporters knew—the relaxed, humorous, sarcastic, down-to-earth person who they saw once the cameras were turned off.[6]

Hillary also devoted a great deal of effort in 1996 to helping her husband's campaign for reelection. She spoke on college campuses, at Democratic benefits, and before women's groups, raising more than 11 million dollars. Bill Clinton easily won reelection over the Republican challenger, former Senate Majority Leader Bob Dole.

FOUR MORE YEARS

Shortly after the election, Hillary made it clear that during her husband's second term she planned to continue her public role as a spokesperson for issues affecting children, women, and families. She convened White House conferences on early childhood development and learning, as well as childcare. She spoke out in support of increasing access to childcare for low-income working families, providing increased after-school programs for older children, expanding Head Start, and providing tax incentives for businesses and universities that invested in childcare.

Hillary focused on women's economic empowerment, promoting equal pay and retirement security. She supported research on pediatric medicines and continued to travel around the world as a visible symbol of the policies she was advocating.

In March 1997, she traveled to Africa, as part of an effort to spotlight self-help efforts supported by American foreign assistance and private charities, as well as to speak out about women's rights and support democracy in a part of the world most Americans knew little about. Chelsea accompanied Hillary as they traveled to Senegal, South Africa, Zimbabwe, Tanzania, Uganda, and the newly formed nation of Eritrea. On March 20, 1997, she spoke at the University of Cape Town, encouraging her audience to continue to press forward: "The world is watching," she said, "and the democratic world stands with you. It has been given to you, as to few other peoples in history, the opportunity to hold in your hands your own futures and the futures and dreams of countless millions of others."[7]

In 1997, Chelsea graduated from Sidwell Friends and prepared for enrollment in Stanford University. Hillary tried hard to mask her disappointment that her daughter had chosen a school 3,000 miles away. After settling her daughter in California, Hillary returned to the White House and once more focused her energy on women's issues. In November 1997, she traveled to Central Asia, Russia, and Ukraine. At a speech in Almaty, Kazakhstan, before the Central Asian Conference on Women in Politics, she noted, "Though we practice different religions, come from different places, and have different histories, we speak that same mother tongue—the language of hope."[8]

In December, Hillary was invited to address the United Nations Economic and Social Council to commemorate the fiftieth anniversary of the United Nations General Assembly Adoption and Proclamation of the Universal Declaration of Human Rights. She spoke passionately in support of human rights:

> . . . by extending the circle of citizenship and human dignity to include everyone without exception, then we have the basis where new worlds of hope can flourish. So let us in this year of commemoration walk toward those new worlds. Let us do so knowing that the path will never be easy. These rights may be eternal, but so too is the struggle to attain them. Though the darkness of the human heart may recede, it will never go away. It must be with realistic eyes that we look for human rights.[9]

A TIME OF TESTING

The path would not be easy for Hillary in early 1998. Special prosecutor Kenneth Starr had continued his investigation into wrongdoing by the Clinton administration, and by early 1998, he had expanded the focus of his investigation to include charges related to the Paula Jones sexual harassment case against Bill Clinton. On January 21, 1998, Hillary learned from her husband that news reports suggested that he had had an intimate relationship with a former White House intern named Monica Lewinsky and then asked her to lie about it to the attorneys representing Paula Jones. He told her that the charges were false; Hillary believed her husband. She felt certain that the charges were part of an attempt to undermine Bill Clinton's legitimacy as president, to "attack him personally when he could not be defeated politically." [10]

Within a week, Hillary appeared on the *Today* show to keep a previously scheduled appointment to drum up support for the president's upcoming State of the Union address. Instead, she was forced to answer questions about the rumors. There, she famously defended her husband with the words, ". . . the great story here for anybody willing to find it and write about it and explain it is this vast right-wing conspiracy that has been conspiring against my husband since the day he announced for president."[11]

Hillary chose to press ahead with her own focus on issues that mattered to her. She organized a series of White House lectures and performances in which historians, scientists, and artists explored a wide range of issues, from American jazz to cosmology to genome research. She initiated Save America's Treasures, a program to restore America's cultural and historic landmarks.

On August 15, 1998, Bill Clinton told Hillary that there was, in fact, more to his relationship with Monica Lewinsky than he had initially admitted. He told her that there had been an inappropriate relationship with the intern and that he was going to have to admit it in his grand jury testimony the next day.

In her memoirs, Hillary admitted the devastation her husband's confession caused: "I couldn't believe what I was hearing. . . . I was dumbfounded, heartbroken and outraged."[12]

IMPEACHMENT

For several months, Hillary coped with the conflicting demands of her personal crisis and her political obligations. She learned in September that Kenneth Starr's office had sent on a referral on impeachment to the House Judiciary Committee, which would then decide whether or not the matter should be referred to the House of Representatives for a vote. Hillary strongly believed that wrong as her husband's behavior had been, it did not constitute a legal basis for impeachment as outlined in the Constitution. She focused on the upcoming midterm elections as a way for the American people to send a message to their representatives and the president—a message supporting Clinton's policies, if not his personal behavior. She spent the fall of 1998 traveling the country, urging people to vote for Democratic candidates. She traveled to California,

President Clinton, seen here with Hillary at a Democratic National Committee dinner on January 15, 1999, shows the strain of fulfilling his elected responsibilities during his Senate trial. It was a tense time for the couple: Bill had originally denied the claims that he had a sexual relationship with a young White House intern named Monica Lewinsky, and Hillary publicly defended his innocence. After an investigation was launched, however, Bill told Hillary that he had lied to her and that the allegations of his affair were in fact true.

Washington State, Illinois, Ohio, Nevada, Arkansas, and Wisconsin. She worked particularly hard on behalf of Representative Charles Schumer in his campaign to defeat New York senator Al D'Amato. She was relieved and happy when the election results showed that the Democrats had gained five additional seats in the House and that Chuck Schumer had defeated Al D'Amato.

A few days after the election, on November 6, 1998, veteran New York senator Daniel Moynihan announced that he would not run for a fifth term. Representative Charlie Rangle, a Congressman from Harlem, quickly placed a call to Hillary, urging Hillary to consider a run for Moynihan's Senate seat. Rangle was not the first person to suggest that Hillary consider a run for the U.S. Senate, but at the time, she dismissed it as a farfetched idea, focusing more on the upcoming impeachment hearings.

In December, the House of Representatives passed two

PRESCRIPTION DRUG COVERAGE

As a senator, Hillary Rodham Clinton continued to focus on the issues that mattered to her. Healthcare proved a key component of the issues with which she was identified, and on June 20, 2003, she spoke out on the floor of the U.S. Senate addressing the issue of Medicare and prescription drugs:

. . . Medicare and Social Security came to be the embodiment of our country's great ideas: if you work hard all of your life and play by the rules you will not be left to fend for yourself in your golden years. If you helped make America stronger, smarter, and better, then the nation would help make your retirement years better, healthier, and more secure.

For those who believe in Social Security and Medicare, this social contract was a fundamental agreement between a country and its citizens. It was not the establishment of an entitlement, but the establishment of a responsibility among generations based on individual, family, and national responsibility.

. . . I propose an amendment that will help consumers in two ways. First, it would ensure research comparing the efficacy and articles of impeachment—those of perjury in the grand jury and obstruction of justice. Bill Clinton next faced a trial in the U.S. Senate, which began on January 7, 1999. Hillary avoided watching the five-week trial on television, convinced that it was a miscarriage of justice but also certain that her husband would be acquitted.

On February 12, 1999, the U.S. Senate voted to acquit Bill Clinton of the impeachment charges. On that same day, Hillary Clinton had a lengthy meeting with Harold Ickes, an expert on New York politics. Many leading Democrats were urging Hillary to consider a run for the Senate, and she had finally decided to consider a campaign—this time of her own.

cost-effectiveness of top drugs used by Medicare and Medicaid beneficiaries. Often there are a number of competing drugs to treat the same condition. But which is more effective? Since drug companies don't always have an incentive to do head-to-head trials of their drug against their competitors, oftentimes we just don't know. But we need to know that we are getting the value for each of our $400 billion.

And second, if we want seniors to make informed choices as consumers, then we should make these comparison studies available to seniors. Drug ads should contain this information, so they don't mislead seniors. We should put this information on the Internet, and we should guarantee that funding for consumer counseling is adequate. . .

Fix the problems now so that later we can focus our efforts on doing more to bring Medicare into the twenty-first century. Our system of helping those in need is itself in need of help.*

* Hillary Rodham Clinton, "Floor Statement of Senator Clinton on Medicare Prescription Drug Proposal," June 20, 2003. *http://clinton.senate.gov*

8

Senator Clinton

Our lives are a mixture of different roles. Most of us are doing the best we can to find whatever the right balance is . . . For me, that balance is family, work, and service.
—Hillary Rodham Clinton, quoted in *Living History*

The offer of a possible seat in the Senate was not the only opportunity presented to Hillary as her husband's second term as president began to draw to a close. Many people approached her with a multitude of offers—some casual, some serious and carefully prepared. There was talk of her heading a foundation or serving as president of a university; she was suggested as a candidate for several different positions in international policymaking—with the United Nations, or as an ambassador, or with the World Bank. She was approached about hosting a television show or becoming a corporate CEO.

Judith Hope, the chairman of the New York Democratic Party, was one of the first to approach Hillary about a run for the Senate seat to be vacated by Daniel Moynihan. Hillary had been considering where she would live after she and Bill left the White House, and New York City was one of the most appealing ideas. She loved the pace of life in New York, its sophistication, and its liberal politics.[1]

Harold Ickes, the New York strategist, explained to Hillary the challenges she would be facing, should she choose to run for the Senate. New York State was far more than New York City. Hillary would need to master the problems confronting its 19 million citizens, not only those in its most glamorous city, but those living in Syracuse and Albany, in Buffalo and Niagara Falls. She would need to travel the state, to meet its people and speak to their concerns. She would need to grasp the economic problems facing upstate New York and the security issues facing Manhattan, to gain a grasp of the local politics in all of its 54,000 square miles.

Ickes pointed out to Hillary the many obstacles she would face. She was not from New York. She had never run for political office. Her opponent would be Rudy Giuliani, the popular mayor of New York City and an experienced politician. She would need to coordinate her campaign with her responsibilities as First Lady.

She spoke with many prominent New Yorkers, including Senator Moynihan and his wife, former New York City Mayors Ed Koch and David Dinkins, Senator Schumer, and Judith Hope. She received their support and encouragement, but many friends discouraged her from the campaign, saying that it would be too grueling, too draining, and the least attractive of her many career options. But many of the issues Hillary cared about were decided in the U.S. Senate. "I had spoken out about the importance of women participating in politics and government," Hillary explained, "seeking elective office and using the power of their own voices to shape public policy and chart their nations' futures. How could I pass up an opportunity to do the same?"[2]

The prospect of a campaign also brought a point of reconciliation to her marriage. Hillary Rodham and Bill Clinton could once more weigh the pros and cons of a campaign, plot strategy and discuss tactics. This time, though, it was Hillary who would do the campaigning.

PLANNING THE RACE

Hillary set a goal of raising $25 million, the amount she felt was necessary for a New York race. She drafted the help of Terry McAuliffe, a friend from Syracuse who was an experienced fundraiser. She formed an exploratory committee in June and began interviewing potential campaign staff. She also began house-hunting in New York State, finally settling on a converted farmhouse in Chappaqua, north of New York City.

On July 7, she launched what she dubbed a "listening tour," a plan to travel around New York and meet with local leaders to better determine the concerns and answer the questions of what she hoped might become her constituents. At the home of Senator Moynihan, she officially announced the formation of her campaign committee, noting her hope that by meeting with the people of New York she might be able to demonstrate "that what I'm from is maybe as important, if not more important, than where I'm from."[3]

The fact that she was not a native New Yorker proved a serious obstacle in the early days of her campaign. Still, Hillary was successful in small crowds. People who had not expected to like her found themselves impressed by her in person. She focused more on grassroots campaigning than giving interviews to the media, understanding that she was more comfortable one-on-one or in small groups than before a sea of microphones and cameras.

In February 2000, Hillary formally declared her candidacy for the Senate in a speech at the State University of New York in Purchase. Her husband, mother, and daughter were all there to cheer her on.

Her advisors had cautioned her that Rudolph Giuliani would be a tough opponent, but Giuliani spent the majority of his time in New York City, and Hillary benefited by underscoring her concern for voters upstate. Two incidents involving fatal shootings of unarmed African Americans by New York City police officers undermined support for Giuliani by the African-American community. Hillary's campaign underscored other issues on which Mayor Giuliani was vulnerable, including coping with the homeless, his grasp of international affairs, the minimum wage, Republican tax cuts, and the Nuclear Test Ban Treaty rejected by the Republican Senate.

Then, on May 19, 2000, Mayor Giuliani made the shocking announcement that he was withdrawing from the senate race. He had recently been diagnosed with prostate cancer, and his troubled marriage was sparking endless stories in the press.

CAMPAIGN CHALLENGES

Giuliani's withdrawal from the Senate race was not a gift to Hillary's campaign. Her advisors had based their strategy largely on Giuliani's strengths and weaknesses. They quickly needed to develop a new plan when the Republican Party announced that its nominee would be Rick Lazio, a 42-year-old Congressman from Long Island. Lazio quickly launched a campaign attacking Clinton. His fundraising letter said that his campaign could be summed up in six words: "I'm running against Hillary Rodham Clinton." The statement was undeniably true, but it gave prospective voters little insight into why they should vote for Lazio, for where he stood on issues, for his accomplishments in Congress, for what he hoped to accomplish in the senate.

On September 13, in Buffalo, Hillary and Lazio appeared for Hillary's first debate as a political candidate. Moderator Tim Russert from NBC proved a tough questioner, producing a tape of her comments about the "right-wing conspiracy" on the *Today* show two years earlier and asking her if she regretted "misleading the American people." Lazio was questioned about his comments that Hillary had "embarrassed our country" and for his links to the more conservative Republicans.

During the campaign, Lazio had raised the issue of "soft money," money raised by independent groups to be used on behalf of candidates. During the debate, Lazio whipped out a piece of paper from his suit jacket, held out a pen in his other hand, and marched across the stage to Hillary. Holding the document only an inch from Hillary's face, he said, "Let's sign it. It's the New York Freedom from Soft Money Pact. I signed it. We can both sit down together. . . let's get it done now. Let's not give any more wiggle room."[4]

Hillary pushed away the document, noting that she admired Lazio for his "performance," and as he returned to his podium she said that she would be happy to sign the pledge, but Lazio continued to berate her, interrupting her each time by saying, "Right here, sign it right now!"[5]

The stunt, intended to demonstrate Lazio's determination to stand up to "soft money" special interests and Hillary Rodham Clinton, backfired. Writer Gail Collins in the New York Times described Lazio's action as "invading her space," while Lars-Erik Nelson of the *New York Daily News* described Lazio's march across the stage as a "childish, contrived stunt."[6] Even Moderator Tim Russert came under fire for dredging up the specter of Monica Lewinsky in a debate that, some said, should have focused on the issues confronting New Yorkers, not on the problems Hillary had experienced in her marriage.

Hillary campaigned hard, answering Lazio's campaign theme of "six words: I'm running against Hillary Rodham Clinton," with the comment that "New Yorkers deserve more than that. How about seven words? How about jobs, education, health, Social Security, environment, choice?"[7]

On election day, November 7, Hillary voted with her husband and daughter in Chappaqua. "After seeing Bill's name

Hillary shakes hands with Congressman Rick Lazio, her Republican challenger, before their debate during the 2000 campaign for one of New York's U.S. Senate seats. Although Hillary was not a native New Yorker, she conducted a "listening tour" to meet with leaders around the state and learn about her potential constituents' concerns. Hillary defeated Lazio, becoming the first former First Lady to hold an elected office.

on the ballots for years, I was thrilled and honored to see my own," she said.[8] The results revealed a large margin of victory, with Hillary winning 55 percent of the vote to Lazio's 43 percent. Hillary Rodham Clinton had become a United States senator from New York.

AN END AND A BEGINNING

On January 20, 2000, Hillary Rodham Clinton said her final good-byes to the White House. She had spent eight long and difficult years there, but she was looking forward to a new chapter: her career as the junior senator from New York.

Her career in the Senate was marked by several triumphs. She was able to champion the causes she has consistently supported: education, women's health, and children's issues. The *Washington Post* described her as "one of the Senate's most prominent and influential Democrats."[9]

In her first two years in office, she worked quietly in a more behind-the-scenes role, learning the traditions and rules of the Senate and focusing on local issues of concern to her

DEMOCRATIC LEADER

On July 29, 2002, Senator Hillary Rodham Clinton spoke at the 2002 Democratic Leadership Council National Convention in New York. It was part of a new platform that expanded Hillary's focus beyond the issues directly affecting New Yorkers to a more national perspective, placing her—some suggested—in line for a future campaign for the presidency.

Her speech provided an opportunity for the senator to link herself with the successes of her husband's presidency—with its time of economic prosperity and with the passage of such bills as the Family Leave Act, the Brady Bill, the Earned Income Tax Credit, and others:

The results speak for themselves. Those ideas were converted into policies and programs that literally changed millions of lives and, I argue, changed America. Twenty-two-and-a-half million new jobs, seven million people out of poverty, 35 million Americans using the Family Medical Leave Act, record home ownership and college enrollment, the lowest crime rate in 27 years and the lowest welfare rolls in 35 years, the lowest minority unemployment on record, and hundreds of billions of constituency. Following the terrorist attacks on New York and Washington on September 11, 2001, Senator Clinton addressed her colleagues, demonstrating the bipartisan unity she felt was critical: "I have expressed my strong support for the president [George W. Bush]. Not only as the senator from New York, but as someone who for eight years has some sense of the burdens and responsibilities that fall on the shoulders of the human being we make our president. It is an awesome and an oftentimes awful responsibility for any person." [10]

After two years, Hillary was chosen to serve as chairman of the Democratic Steering Committee, a Senate organization that helps promote the party's agenda. Hillary quickly demonstrated energy and skill at encouraging party activists and

dollars were used to pay down the national debt, and we had the first three surpluses in a row in more than 70 years . . .

Notice the balance, the equilibrium, that exists between society and government in the Democratic notion of responsibility. Demands are made, and rewards are given. There is connectivity, a cause and effect, that forms the basis of the social compact that makes America so unique and so great. There is something behind these ideals; they're not just one-time feel good, sound good, sound bytes. They're rooted in a good understanding of human nature— how the private and public sector each needs to do its part to move people forward. And the way our country needs to feel that the game is not rigged. That we all have a chance . . .

If we take that message to the electorate, I believe that we're going to be successful and we have an opportunity to be the majority party once again, in the Congress, in the state legislatures, and eventually in the White House. *

* http://clinton.senate.gov

enlisting their support of Democratic candidates. She proved skillful at campaigning and fundraising for members of her party. In 2002, she was one of only six Democrats awarded the Golden Gavel for presiding over the Senate for more than 100 hours. She was appointed to several influential committees, including Environment and Public Works; Health, Education, Labor and Pensions; and the Armed Services Committee (she was the first New Yorker elected to this committee).

The publication of her autobiography, *Living History*, in 2003 marked a new phase in her career. Once more she answered questions about her time in the White House, her marriage, and her past, but the national tour to promote the book also provided her with a forum to discuss her ideas and policies on a national platform. It is not surprising that Hillary was soon being asked whether or not she would consider becoming a candidate for president in 2004. Hillary Rodham Clinton made it clear that she had no plans to run in 2004 and instead intended to serve her full six-year term in the Senate.

Her six-year term will expire in 2006, and many believe that she will then become a candidate for the presidency. She is becoming increasingly involved in shaping the Democratic Party's ideas and policies; it is not difficult to speculate that she might seek to further her ideas as president.

"I'm flattered that the question gets asked," Hillary said in a 2003 interview with ABC's Barbara Walters, ". . . and I hope that it will lead to a woman running for president, and we have a lot of good women."[11] As a senior in high school, Hillary ran for student government president, an election she lost. One of her opponents told her that she was "really stupid" if she thought that "a girl could be elected president."[12] Yet now, the woman most voters consider as the most likely candidate to become the first woman president of the United States is Hillary Rodham Clinton.

Hillary Rodham Clinton remains a polarizing figure. A Gallup Poll, conducted May 30–June 1, 2003, showed that

33 percent of those polled felt that she was qualified to serve as president and that they would vote for her, and 44 percent felt that she was not qualified. The poll showed an even split, with 43 percent of those polled having both "favorable" and "unfavorable" opinions of Hillary Rodham Clinton.[13]

Eleanor Roosevelt described the constraints she experienced while First Lady, and the sense of freedom that came with stepping out of that role: "It was almost as though I had erected someone a little outside of myself who was the president's wife. I was lost somewhere deep down inside myself. That is the way I felt and worked until I left the White House."[14]

"I wasn't born a First Lady or a senator," Hillary noted in her autobiography. She continued:

I wasn't born a Democrat. I wasn't born a lawyer or an advocate for women's rights and human rights. I wasn't born a wife or mother. I was born an American in the middle of the twentieth century, a fortunate time and place. I was free to make choices unavailable to past generations of women in my own country and inconceivable to many women in the world today. I came of age on the crest of tumultuous social change and took part in the political battles fought over the meaning of America and its role in the world.[15]

Chronology

1947   Hillary Rodham is born on October 26.

1968   Hillary interns at House Republican Conference in Washington, D.C.

1969   Hillary graduates from Wellesley College and becomes college's first student commencement speaker.

1971   Hillary meets Bill Clinton while at Yale Law School.

1973   Hillary takes a job with the Children's Defense Fund.

1974   Hillary joins House Judiciary Committee's staff investigating impeachment charges against President Richard Nixon.

1975   Hillary moves to Arkansas and marries Bill Clinton.

1976   The Clintons move to Little Rock. Hillary joins Rose Law Firm.

1978   Bill Clinton is elected governor. Bill and Hillary form land development partnership known as Whitewater Development Company with Jim and Susan McDougal.

1979   Hillary becomes partner at Rose Law.

1980   Hillary gives birth to daughter Chelsea. Bill Clinton loses his reelection campaign.

1981   Hillary begins using her husband's name, becoming Hillary Rodham Clinton.

1982   Bill Clinton again becomes governor. Hillary is chosen to head educational reform initiative.

1991   Bill Clinton launches his campaign for presidency.

1992   Bill Clinton is elected president. Hillary becomes chair of Task Force on National Healthcare Reform. Hugh Rodham dies.

1993   Hillary testifies before Congress in September as lead witness in healthcare initiative.

1994   The healthcare plan fails passage by Congress. A special prosecutor is appointed to investigate Whitewater.

1995 Hillary attends UN Fourth World Conference on Women in China.

1996 *It Takes a Village* is published. Hillary testifies before a grand jury. Bill Clinton is reelected.

1998 New York Democratic leaders urge Hillary run for the Senate.

1999 Impeachment trial of Bill Clinton in the Senate; he is ultimately acquitted. Hillary begins a "listening tour" to explore Senate run.

2000 Hillary is elected to the U.S. Senate on November 7.

2002 Hillary becomes chairman of Democratic Steering Committee. She wins the Golden Gavel.

2003 Her autobiography, *Living History,* is published and becomes a national bestseller.

Notes

CHAPTER 1:

1 Sidney Blumenthal, *The Clinton Wars*. New York: Farrar, Straus, Giroux, 2003, p. 699.

2 Hillary Rodham Clinton, *Remarks and Commentary: Vital Voices 1997–1999*. Washington, D.C.: Executive Office of the President, pp. 66–67.

3 Mary Matalin and James Carville, *All's Fair: Love, War and Running for President*. New York: Random House, 1994, p. 476.

CHAPTER 2:

1 Hillary Clinton, *It Takes a Village*. New York: Simon & Schuster, 1996, p. 25.

2 Gail Sheehy, *Hillary's Choice*. New York: Random House, 1999, p. 24.

3 Ibid.

4 Clinton, *It Takes a Village*, p. 153.

5 Joyce Milton, *The First Partner: Hillary Rodham Clinton*. New York: William Morrow, 1999, p. 13.

6 Ibid.

7 Clinton, *It Takes a Village*, pp. 23–24.

8 Ibid., p. 22

9 Milton, *The First Partner*, p. 16.

10 Clinton, *It Takes a Village*, p. 27.

11 Ibid., p. 29.

12 Sheehy, *Hillary's Choice*, p. 37.

13 Ibid., p. 39.

CHAPTER 3:

1 Clinton, *Living History*, p. 27.

2 Ibid., p. 38

3 Ibid., p. 40

4 Ibid, p. 41

5 Donnie Radcliffe, *Hillary Rodham Clinton*. New York: Warner Books, 1993, p. 83.

6 Roger Morris, *Partners in Power*. New York: Henry Holt, 1996, p. 137.

7 Ibid., p. 142.

8 Ibid., p. 143.

9 Clinton, *Living History*, p. 52.

10 Ibid.

11 Ibid.

12 Radcliffe, *Hillary Rodham Clinton*, p. 112.

13 Clinton, *Living History*, pp. 59–60.

14 Ibid., p. 61.

15 Radcliffe, *Hillary Rodham Clinton*, p. 118.

CHAPTER 4 :

1 Clinton, *Living History*, p. 69.

2 Ibid.

3 Ibid., p. 70.

4 Milton, *The First Partner: Hillary Rodham Clinton*, p. 85.

5 Gail Sheehy, *Hillary's Choice*, p. 123.

6 Ibid.

7 Clinton, *Living History*, p. 75.

8 Ibid., p. 82.

9 Milton, *The First Partner: Hillary Rodham Clinton*, p. 102.

10 Clinton, *Living History*, p. 88.

11 Id., *It Takes a Village*, p. 70.

12 Id., *Living History*, p. 92.

13 Ibid., p. 93.

CHAPTER 5:

1 Sheehy, *Hillary's Choice*, p. 145.

2 Ibid., p. 152.

3 Clinton, *Living History*, p. 95.

4 Ibid., p. 100.

5 Ibid., pp. 102–3.

6 Matalin and Carville, *All's Fair: Love, War and Running for President*, p. 88.

7 Clinton, *Living History*, p. 105.

8 Sheehy, *Hillary's Choice*, p. 209.

9 Milton, *The First Partner*, p. 221.

10 Sheehy, *Hillary's Choice*, p. 210.

11 Clinton, *Living History*, p. 110.

12 Id., *It Takes a Village*, p. 211.

13 Sheehy, *Hillary's Choice*, p. 219.

14 Eleanor Roosevelt, *This I Remember*. New York: Harper & Brothers, 1949, p. 89.

15 Clinton, *Living History*, p. 138.

16 Hillary Rodham Clinton, *Remarks by First Lady Hillary Rodham Clinton, United Nations Fourth World Conference on Women, September 5–6, 1995*. Washington, D.C.: Executive Office of the President, p. 4.

17 Clinton, *Living History*, p. 148.

CHAPTER 6:

1 Roosevelt, *This I Remember*, p. 7.

2 George Stephanopoulos, *All Too Human*. Boston: Little, Brown, 1999, p. 198.

3 Clinton, *Living History*, p. 153.

4 Ibid., p. 161.

5 Ibid., p. 179.

6 Stephanopoulos, *All Too Human*, p. 202.

7 Clinton, *Living History*, p. 189.

8 Stephanopoulos, *All Too Human*, p. 301.

9 Sheehy, *Hillary's Choice*, p. 255.

CHAPTER 7:

1 Clinton, *Living History*, p. 213.

2 Sheehy, *Hillary's Choice*, p. 265.

3 Clinton, *It Takes A Village*, p. 14.

4 Id., *Remarks at the United Nations Fourth World Conference on Women, September 5–6, 1995*, p. 1.

5 Ibid., p. 6.

6 Sheehy, *Hillary's Choice*, p. 291.

7 Hillary Rodham Clinton, *Remarks and Commentary by First Lady Hillary Rodham Clinton, Central Asia, Russia, Ukraine*. Washington, D.C.: Executive Office of the President, 1997, p. 5.

8 Ibid., p. 13.

9 Hillary Rodham Clinton, *Remarks and Commentary on the Fiftieth Anniversary of the United Nations General Assembly Adoption and Proclamation of the Universal Declaration of Human Rights*. Washington, D.C.: Executive Office of the President, 1997, p. 8.

10 Id., *Living History*, p. 443.

11 Ibid., p. 445.

12 Ibid., p. 466.

CHAPTER 8:

1 Sheehy, *Hillary's Choice*, p. 334.

2 Clinton, *Living History*, p. 502.

3 Ibid., p. 507.

Notes

4 Blumenthal, *The Clinton Wars*, p. 696.

5 Michael Tomasky, *Hillary's Turn*. New York: The Free Press, 2001, p. 238.

6 Ibid., p. 239.

7 Ibid., p. 255.

8 Clinton, *Living History*, p. 523.

9 Jim Vandehei, "Clinton Develops into a Force in the Senate," *The Washington Post*. 5 March 2003, p. A1.

10 Hillary Rodham Clinton, "Statement on the Senate Floor In Response to the World Trade Center and Pentagon Attacks." 12 September 2001. Senator Hillary Rodham Clinton's Website. *<http://clinton.senate.gov/~clinton/news/2001/09/2001912D06.html>*.

11 "Hillary: No Intention of Running for President." CNN.com, 9 June 2003. *<http://www.cnn.com/2003/ALLPOLITICS/06/08/hillary>*.

12 Clinton, *Living History*, p. 24.

13 Gallup Poll, "Hillary Clinton Remains a Polarizing Figure." *The PlainDealer*, 14 June 2003, p. B9.

14 Roosevelt, *This I Remember*, pp. 350–351.

15 Clinton, *Living History*, p. 1.

Blumenthal, Sidney. *The Clinton Wars*. New York: Farrar, Straus and Giroux, 2003.

Clinton, Hillary Rodham. *It Takes a Village*. New York: Simon and Schuster, 1996.

———. *Living History*. New York: Simon and Schuster, 2003.

———. *Remarks and Commentary on Africa*. Washington, D.C.: Executive Office of the President, 1997.

———. *Remarks and Commentary on Central Asia, Russia, Ukraine*. Washington, D.C.: Executive Office of the President 1997.

———. *Remarks at the United Nations Fourth World Conference on Women. September 5–6, 1995*. Washington, D.C.: Executive Office of the President, 1995.

———. *Remarks in Commemoration of the Fiftieth Anniversary of the United Nations General Assembly Adoption and Proclamation of the Universal Declaration of Human Rights*. Washington, D.C.: Executive Office of the President, 1997.

———. *Remarks and Commentary, Vital Voices, 1997–1999*. Washington, D.C.: Executive Office of the President, 1999.

Gallup poll. "Hillary Clinton Remains a Polarizing Figure," *The Plain Dealer*, 14 June 2003, sec. B.

Hernandez, Raymond. "Book Gives Mrs. Clinton a New Turn in Spotlight," *New York Times*, 9 June 2003. Available online through the archives at *http://www.nytimes.com/*.

Maraniss, David. "First Lady's Determination Binds Power Partnership," *Washington Post*, 1 February 1998, sec. A.

Merida, Kevin. "The First Lady Forges On," *Washington Post*, 20 September 1998, sec. A.

Matalin, Mary, and James Carville. *All's Fair: Love, War and Running for President*. New York: Random House, 1994.

Milton, Joyce. *The First Partner: Hillary Rodham Clinton*. New York: William Morrow, 1999.

Morris, Roger. *Partners in Power*. New York: Henry Holt, 1996.

Nagourney, Adam, and Raymond Hernandez. "Their Lives an Open Book, Clintons Enter a New Phase," *New York Times*, 5 June 2003. Available online through the archives at *http://www.nytimes.com/*.

Radcliffe, Donnie. *Hillary Rodham Clinton*. New York: Warner Books, 1993.

Bibliography

Roosevelt, Eleanor. *This I Remember.* New York: Harper & Brothers, 1949.

Sheehy, Gail. *Hillary's Choice.* New York: Random House, 1999.

Stephanopoulos, George. *All Too Human.* Boston: Little, Brown, 1999.

Tomasky, Michael. *Hillary's Turn.* New York: The Free Press, 2001.

Vandehei, Jim. "Clinton develops into a force in the Senate," *Washington Post,* 5 March 2003, sec. A1.

Woodward, Bob. *The Choice.* New York: Simon and Schuster, 1996.

Websites:

20/20 Interactive: "Immediate Attraction"
http://www.abcnews.go.com/sections/2020/US/
    hillary_walters030608.html

Bartleby.com
http://www.bartleby.com

Children's Defense Fund
http://www.childrensdefense.org

Senator Hillary Rodham Clinton's Website
http://www.clinton.senate.gov

CNN.com: "Potential Candidate Hillary Clinton Readies
    for New York Blitz"
http://www.cnn.com/allpolitics/stories/1999/07/04/
    hillary.senate/

New York Times
http://www.nytimes.com

American Experience: The Presidents
http://www.pbs.org/wgbh/amex/presidents

The Washington Post
http://www.washingtonpost.com

Watergate.info: Watergate—The Scandal that Brought Down
    Richard Nixon
http://www.watergate.info

About.com: Women's History
http://www.womenshistory.about.com

Books

Bartley, Robert L. (ed.). *Whitewater: From the Editorial Pages of the Wall Street Journal.* New York: Dow Jones and Company, 1994.

Clinton, Hillary Rodham. *An Invitation to the White House.* New York: Simon and Schuster, 2000.

Halley, Patrick S. *On the Road with Hillary: A Behind-the-Scenes Look at the Journey from Arkansas to the U.S. Senate.* New York: Viking Press, 2002.

Harpaz, Beth J. *The Girls in the Van: Covering Hillary.* New York: St. Martin's Press, 2001.

Laskas, Jeanne Marie and Lynn Johnson. *We Remember: Women Born at the Turn of the Century Tell the Stories of their Lives in Words and Pictures.* New York: Hearst Books, 1999.

Web

Senator Hillary Rodham Clinton's Website
http://www.clinton.senate.gov

The Empire Page
http://www.empirepage.com

New York Times
http://www.nytimes.com

The White House
http://www.whitehouse.gov

About.com: Women's History
http://www.womenshistory.about.com

Index

Index

Index

Credits

About the Author

Heather Lehr Wagner is a writer and editor. She earned an M.A. in government from the College of William and Mary and a B.A. in political science from Duke University. She is the author of more than 20 books for teens, including explorations of people in conflict and the creation of the modern Middle East, and biographies of great American presidents and extraordinary women.